RELEASED
FROM THE PRISON MY FATHER BUILT

by JAMES RYLE

Published by

Truth*Works*
Helping You Experience God's Presence

Printed in the United States of America
International Standard Book Number: 978-0-9826144-0-2
Library of Congress cataloging-in-publishing data
available upon request.

Truth*Works*
P.O.Box 469
Franklin TN 37065
Phone: 615.595.8691

website: www.truthworks.org

Unless otherwise noted in the end-notes, all Scripture quotations
are from the King James Version of the Bible.

First printing, January 2010

"If I have seen farther than others, it is because I was standing on the shoulders of giants."

Sir Isaac Newton[1]

Thank you to all the giants who have carried me on their strong shoulders these several years. I would have never made it this far without you, and could never have told my story as I do in these pages. To God be the glory, but all praise belongs to you. In the words of Robert Burton, "I light my candle by your torches."[2]

James Ryle

Table of Contents

Author's Note

*F*irst, I make a humble appeal to the well-read ladies of our world. This book is for *every* man in your life. It is for your father, brother, and son; for your uncle, cousin, and friend. It is for your employer, co-worker, or your employees.

For this reason I ask you to please bear with my decision to write this book as a man speaking to men. That's not to say there is nothing here for you, for I know you will be able to read between the lines and find those truths that are common to us all – men and women alike.

However, I wrote specifically to men so as not to risk missing my target by generalizing the topic. I'm aiming so as to hit your man square in the heart. And the benefits of that singular strike will be yours forever!

And now a word to the man who holds this book in his hands. You are an endangered species. Over the past forty years a relentless assault against men has wrecked havoc upon our sense of self-worth. We have been mocked and jeered, ridiculed and marginalized. Our ranks have been diminished and our fraternity has all but faded into the pages of history. We have ventured through the terrain of the changing social landscape like nomads in search of our souls; loners in quest of a Tribe.

And our families have suffered the fallout of the body blows that have landed upon us. Divorce is skyrocketing, children are fatherless, boys are lost in the fog – and most of us as men are dazed with shell shock.

But no more. This book is for you. Its message is one of hope and recovery. It represents the dawn of a new day; the promise of a brighter tomorrow.

What you will read and discover in the following pages will aid you in becoming the husband your wife yearns for, the father your children look up to, and the man you've always dreamed of being – a good neighbor, a great brother, a true friend, a noble citizen, a better man.

This book will help you experience the presence of God and find the power He provides for you to be who He has called you to be, and to do what He has created you to do. Yours will be a life lived to the glory of God. And what a sight that will be!

"All creation waits eagerly for the sons of God to be revealed" (Romans 8:19). Yes, our world is waiting on *you*!

"Hey, Ryle, how long did it take you to write this?" a friend asked after reading the manuscript for this book. *"So far, about forty years,"* I answered.

So, this is my story, but it is one that's still unfolding. I thought it would be good to at least pause for a moment and post what I've discovered along the way, for other travelers such as you.

Thankfully, it will not take you forty years to read it! However, I pray that the message herein will last you a lifetime – and *beyond*. For I write with eternity in mind.

JAMES RYLE
January 2010

Chapter One

A Life-changing Conversation
With a Guy Named Bert

W e've all experienced it countless times. We dial a number; hear the ring tone, and then someone on the other end answers, "Hello." But this phone call was different. The voice that answered was my father, and we had not spoken in many years.

"Is this Bert Ryle?" I asked.

"Yes it is," he answered.

"Bert *Eugene* Ryle?" I asked specifically.

"Yes it is," he replied, with growing curiosity in his voice.

"Is this the Bert Eugene Ryle who has a son named *James*?" I then asked pointedly.

He paused for a guarded moment, and then cautiously replied, "Yes it is."

"Well, dad, this is *James*."

There was halting silence on the other end. It was brief, but felt like forever. I could tell that he didn't know what to say, so I continued, "This isn't one of those phone calls where you owe me something. I'm not calling to unload on you in any way. I'm grown up; I'm married, and have kids. I'm a father; you're a grandfather. I'm just calling to see if there's any chance that we can get together, that's it. If you say no, you'll never hear from me again."

And then I added, "But please don't say no."

Dad paused again, and then said, "I think that would be good, son. I'd love to see you."

It took us a few weeks to plan our trip from Denver to Houston, and two days to actually make the drive. But the knock on that door was the final step in a journey that had taken twenty-six years. Little did I know that once the door opened another journey would begin - and that would be the journey of a lifetime.

I had long carried a question in the back of my mind. I needed an answer, and dad was the only person who could give it. But we didn't know each other. All of that was about to change on the other side of that door.

I took a deep breath and slowly let it out, then rang the doorbell. I heard footsteps, watched as the doorknob turned, and looked up to see my father standing there before me.

He had a face that looked like a basset hound; sad and sagging ever downward. It was obvious he had not laughed in years. He sported a marine crew cut, which went well with his sleeveless t-shirt and khaki pants. And though in his seventies, he still had good muscles and a strong grip. He also had large ears; he looked like a Volkswagen with the doors open. I couldn't help but wonder, "Is this what I'm going to look like when I get old?"

"Welcome son," dad said with a thick Texas drawl. "Y'all come on in."

The first few days of our visit were understandably awkward for not only Belinda and me, along with our kids, but also for dad. After all, we were virtual strangers. Still, dad did everything he could to make us feel at ease, and we did the same for him. One evening a few days into our visit as dad and I sat alone in the den, I decided that it was time to ask him my question. But I didn't want to be tactless, so I set it up with another question first.

"Dad, what's your story?" I began, "How did you get from there to here; and where was there, and where is here? All I know is that you were in prison; I really don't know anything else about you." What he said next dropped my jaw to the floor.

"Well, son, when I was a young man I was called into the ministry."

It was the *way* he said it that stunned me - "called into the ministry." That's not something someone casually says. In fact, no one would even think to say such a thing unless it was true.

"Why didn't you do that?" I asked a bit bewildered.

"I really wanted to," he replied, "but I made a stupid choice; I went the wrong way. That led to another stupid choice, and then another...and another."

I could see the reflective remorse on his face as he finally summed it up with these sobering words, "Hell, son; you're looking at a man whose life has been one stupid choice after the next. That's my story."

I was taken back for two reasons. One, is that I would have never imagined that my father had any inclination whatsoever toward God, given his bungled career as a criminal. And, two, I myself was in the ministry, and my dad was unaware of that fact.

"Dad, I am *in* the ministry," I said, still surprised by his words.

"You are *not*," he answered.

"It's *true*, dad; I pastor a church in Colorado."

This time it was my dad who was stunned. Then it struck me that God had set this moment up and was about to do something remarkable.

"Think about this, dad. If you had said yes to God and served Him in ministry, our family would've stayed together. I would've grown up watching you serve God, and then when the time came for me to answer the call; I would have followed your example. And I would be serving God today."

I paused for a moment to let what I was saying sink in, and then said, "Well, I am serving God today – so, even though you didn't follow God's call, God stepped in and made it work out according to His plan anyway. So we're sort of back on track here, dad."

Emboldened by dad's obvious interest I then seized upon the moment and said, "Dad, it's not too late for you. Even though you've made, as you say, a lot of stupid choices; it's not too late for you to make a right one - you can still say yes to God."

> **"It's not too late for you to say *yes* to God."**

Dad did so that night. At the age of seventy-one he gave his heart to Jesus, and spent the remaining five years of his life loving and serving the Lord as best he could. He also tried to sing, but that's another matter.

I can tell you, however, that no hound dog ever sounded so smitten as did my father when he tilted back his ancient head and belted out the old Gospel hymn with deep-toned marine gusto, *"Why Should He Love Me So."* It was nothing any producer would ever push to the market, but I know that when dad sang it, it went straight to the heart of God.

Shortly before he passed away in 1986, dad asked me if I would do him the honor of preaching at his funeral. Of course I said yes. And while dad's friends were touched with the tenderness of my remarks on that day, none of them had any idea of how God had brought my father and me back together on that night when I asked him that first question.

And, amazing as his answer was, it paled in comparison to his answer when I asked him the *next* question. It was the one question that had lingered in the back of my mind ever since I had served time myself in the Texas State Penitentiary.

It was this question which prompted the initial phone call that reconnected me to my dad in the first place. It was the question that would change my life in remarkable ways, and reorder my path with a profound sense of purpose.

Chapter Two

The One Question I Had to Ask

The time was right for me to ask it. My dad and I both had just shared a God-moment together, which seemed to narrow the vast gap that had separated us over the years. On that evening as we sat together in mutual amazement at how God was at work in our lives, we were father and son. And it was wonderful. But it was about to become even more so when my dad answered the next question.

"Dad, which prison were you in?"

Perhaps I should take a minute and explain just why this question weighed so heavily on my mind. You should know that Texas actually has *several* prison units scattered throughout the state, all under the administration of the Texas Department of Corrections, as it was called back then. I had been incarcerated in the state penitentiary at the age of nineteen, and the path that led me there was almost predictable.

I was two years old when dad was arrested and convicted on two counts of armed robbery, and sent to prison. It was a wound that my mother, Ethel Erlene Ryle, would not recover from for years.

Mom put all five of us in a children's home near Round Rock, Texas. I don't remember much about the place, except that it was cold and lonely. We were there for about a year or so it seemed, when mom came and took us back home. As it turned out, this would be short-lived. She had remarried and her new husband was "test-driving" the brood. Evidently he didn't like the way it handled.

The only memories I have of the following few years are disjointed and dark. Jim, my stepfather, was an angry man and it didn't take much to set him off, especially when he had been drinking. And he was *always* drinking. I remember mom taking us kids and hiding in one motel after another, peering through the blinds to see him driving by looking for us.

Somewhere in all this my two older brothers had left. They returned to the children's home in Round Rock, where they had made friends during our earlier visit. That left mom and the remaining three of us, on the run from angry Jim.

Her final option was to do the one thing no mother would ever want to do. She placed us in an orphanage just east of Dallas, different from where my two older brothers were. I'll tell you more about the orphanage a little later, but for now let me just say that it was no place any kid should be *ever*.

I was following in my father's footsteps, and didn't even know it.

It was much too big. It housed in its many dormitories over a thousand kids, ranging in ages from five years old to eighteen. The size alone created an impersonal environment that left a lot of room for the important things in a kid's development to fall between the cracks. Not a lot of nurture, not a lot of affection, and far too much punishment; *abusive* punishment.

So, during my teen years, I ran away. It was a stupid choice; the first of many. Indeed, over the ensuing years I would make one stupid choice after the next, just like dad had done. It seemed, in retrospect, that I was following in my father's footsteps and didn't even know it.

"Wise friends make you wise," Solomon wrote, *"but you hurt yourself by going around with fools."* (Proverbs 13:20)

Being a runaway left me wide open to all sorts of influences, and I gravitated toward the wrong set of friends. It was another stupid choice. I fell into a downward spiral of drugs and rebellion, which came to a disastrous end in a tragic car wreck in the early dawn hours on a long stretch of Texas Farm Road 157, between Euless and Lewisville, on Labor Day weekend 1969.

I fell asleep while driving and crashed into a bridge. A friend who was a passenger in my car lay dead on the highway, and it was my fault. I was arrested and charged with negligent homicide, and faced the possibility of up to three years behind bars. Desperate to get out of trouble, I turned to my friends for advice. Another stupid choice.

Let me offer you a helpful tip - if you are in trouble with the law, do *not* seek legal counsel from hippies! I did so, and my troubles only multiplied.

At their encouragement I started selling drugs in an attempt to make a load of money so I could hire a lawyer who would help me plead my case in court. Hopefully he would be able to use the orphan story and persuade the judge to have mercy on me and let me out of the trouble I was in. *It didn't work.*

Before I could put my plan in motion I was arrested and charged with sales and possession of marijuana, a felony offense that all but guaranteed I was headed for prison.

I was locked up in the Dallas County Jail waiting to find out what they were going to do to me, filled with fear and sinking deeper and deeper into a very real sense of hopelessness. I knew I was in serious trouble, and there was no way out.

One man in jail had been arrested for possessing a single joint, one puff of marijuana, and they gave him five years in prison. Another man had been caught with an ounce of the stuff, and they gave him eight years. Yet another guy had been arrested for selling two ounces and they gave him *fifty* years. That's ten, twenty, thirty, forty, *fifty* years!

They caught me with a full pound of marijuana, half of which was in my possession. I had sold the other half to a guy who led them to me as part of a plea bargain for himself. Like I said, I knew I was in serious trouble. But what I did not know was that God was about to show Himself to me in my darkest moment.

It happened quite unexpectedly. As I stood in the midst of fear and despair, trying to find an answer as to why this was happening to me, a Bible verse I heard as a kid in the orphanage came inexplicably into my mind like a burst of light.

"We know that all things work together for good, to those who love God and are the called according to His purpose." (Romans 8:28)

At the time, I did not fully appreciate as I do now the full implications of that single verse, but in that moment all those years ago it flooded my troubled heart with an unmistakable feeling of hope.

Somehow I sensed that God was saying to me, "I have a purpose for your life, and if you will say yes and stop trying to do things on your own I will work all this out in a way that will astound you." It is to this day one of the most unforgettable moments I've ever experienced. Of course I said yes, and waited with great anticipation for what would happen next.

And I didn't have long to wait.

A portly and disheveled attorney from the public defender's office arrived to meet with me a few days later.

"I've been appointed by the fine state of Texas to represent you," he said, "and I'm good; real good. But I'm not *that* good!" That got my attention.

"You're guilty, and everybody knows it. We've got you, got the evidence, got the witness, got the confession, got the case all nailed down. What we don't have is the time to take this into the court and tie up taxpayer's dollars and juror's time to prove what we all know is true.

"So, acting on your behalf I have talked to the judge, and he assured me that if I can convince you to not fight this in court, the judge said he would give you two years in the state penitentiary."

He then took his glasses off, leaned forward as if to make his point stronger, and said, "Young man, I advise you to take his offer."

I knew that my life was firmly in God's hands.

I could hardly believe what he was saying. I had feared I would be sent to prison for almost a lifetime, and here the man was telling me it would be two years. God had intervened, and started working things together for my good. In that moment I felt a surge of faith and hope, and I knew that my life was firmly in God's hands. Somehow everything was going to be different now. I just *knew* it.

I entered into the prison with a strong awareness of God's presence with me, and a reassuring sense of His protection over me. The Bible, which I had spurned from my childhood days in the orphanage, now became a trusted guide as I walked the dark corridors and stern confines of maximum security. Days turned to weeks, and weeks to months, and always, amidst the clamor of prison chatter, the burden of prison labor, and the emptiness of prison life, I found a deepening friendship with Jesus through the pages of the Bible, and the fellowship of the Holy Spirit.

One night, about a year into my sentence, I was in my cell praying. I simply asked the Lord if I could go home early. "You know better than me what's best," I said, "and You are working all things together for my good. So whatever You decide is fine with me. But if it's OK to ask, can I go home? Could You help me parole out, rather than serve out my entire sentence?"

Upon saying the Amen, I randomly opened my Bible to read from it, and my eyes fell upon this sentence.

"Go home to thy friends, and tell them what great things the Lord has done for thee." (Mark 5:19).

This verse sent a charge through me like electricity; you know, that feeling you get when a chill runs down your spine and goosebumbs flood your skin.

I felt as if the Lord Himself was saying those words to me right then in my cell, and a strong assurance took hold of my heart. I knew two things for sure as I knelt in my prison cell that night. I knew that I was going home, and I knew God wanted me to tell others the story of what He was doing in my life.

To be sure there was no way that I could make this happen myself. I mean, standing in my cell and calling out to the guards to let me out because God told me to go home – well, let's just say that was not going to work! So, if God were *really* speaking to me, then *He* would have to be the one to make it happen. And to my amazement, within one week He did!

I was paroled out of prison, and I set forth on my quest to tell as many people as possible about the goodness of the Lord. Little did I know that one of those people would be my own father. Sitting with him in his den that summer night in Houston, seeing him open his heart back to the Lord made it all worthwhile.

So when I asked him the question, it was with real anticipation in his answer. I was actually hoping that he would say he was in the same prison that I had been in. *Now that would be an amazing story*, I had often thought to myself.

"Dad, which prison were you in?" I asked, leaning forward to hear him say what I already imagined the answer would be. But I was wrong. His answer left me quite disappointed – that is, until I answered a question he then asked me.

Chapter Three

The One Answer I Never Expected

D ad, which prison were you in?"

"I was in the Central Unit," he replied, unaware of all that was lingering behind my question. The moment I heard his answer my countenance dropped. It was *not* the same prison unit I had been in. I had thought for sure it was going to be the same, and had envisioned preaching rousing sermons about being in the same prison that your father was in; you know, the old "like father, like son" thing. But none of this mattered now. His answer changed all that.

"Which prison were *you* in?" he then asked me, not knowing how my mind was racing.

Somewhat dejected I replied, "I was in the Ferguson Unit, near Midway, Texas; just down a ways from Huntsville."

My dad's expression changed immediately. He went from being curious, to being stunned. His mouth dropped open, and he looked at me in disbelief. Gathering himself he then said the words that would forever mark my life.

"Dear God, son, I *built* that prison."

"What?" I replied, "What do you mean, *you* built it?"

"They used prison labor to build the Ferguson Unit," dad answered. "I was the welder on the work crew. I welded the bars when that prison was built."

As dad's words hung there in the air, the Lord Jesus spoke to my heart, "James, I have set you free from the prison your father built. Now I will use you to set others free from prisons their fathers have built. Go home to your friends and tell them what great things I have done. Tell them how all things work together for good for those who love Me and are called according to My purpose."

My mind raced back over the years and grappled with the astounding thought that the Lord had somehow *orchestrated* this entire matter. No, He didn't make my dad a robber, nor did He make me a drug dealer; and the tragic wreck wasn't His doing, it was mine. And He didn't want me to run away from the orphanage, but I did it anyway.

> **"I have set you free from the prison your father built."**

God does no evil to any man; rather, He is the God who works all things after the counsel of His will; the God who works all things - yes, even *bad* things - together for good for those who answer the call to His higher purpose for their lives. And He had been at work in my life all those years even though I didn't know it.

I sat there amazed, and am still so to this very day. My father welded the bars of my prison. How extraordinary is *that?* From one point of view it is very extraordinary. I mean, what are the chances of that ever happening to *anybody?* Extraordinary indeed.

But, from another point of view it is rather ordinary; in fact, it is sadly common. Virtually everywhere in today's world there are sons and daughters in prisons of one kind or another, which their fathers have built. Prisons of fear, addiction, rage, hatred, ignorance, shame, and confusion; just to name a few.

A dad mistreats or neglects a trusting child, and the strike upon that tender soul is as solid and lasting as the iron bars that were welded by the heat of my father's torch. A cruel word spoken in anger, a nickname given in jest, a rebuke blurted out in public or a cold shoulder in time of need – these mindless acts of senseless dads forge the framework of solitary confinement for boys and girls the world over. And the vicious cycle repeats as these wounded children become broken parents with "welding torches" in *their* hands, passing on the torment to yet another generation of unsuspecting kids.

A father's influence in his children's lives is powerful and inevitable, whether for good or for bad. This fact has been repeated throughout history time and time again.

One provocative example of this comes from none other than father Abraham himself. While passing through the land of Egypt, inhabited by pagans who had no regard for God, Abraham decided to lie about Sarah being his wife. His motive was one of self-preservation.

> **A father's influence in his children's lives is powerful and inevitable, whether for good or for bad.**

"You are a beautiful woman," he said to Sarah. "When the Egyptians see you they're going to kill me and take you. Do me a favor: tell them you're my sister, and they will welcome me and let me live" (Gen 12:11-13). Sure enough that's exactly what happened.

The men of that place welcomed Abraham just as he expected, and they took Sarah to be one of Pharaoh's concubines!

God mercifully intervened by disturbing Pharaoh with a frightening dream; the rattled ruler returned Sarah to Abraham and then made them both leave the country.

You think Abraham would have learned from this that he could trust the Lord, being such a great man of faith, but he did the same thing once again while passing through the land of Gerar! And once again God intervened. But here's the more remarkable aspect of this entire story. Some twenty years or so later Isaac, Abraham's son, did the exact same thing, in the exact same place, for the exact same reason! Like father; like son!

Samuel, the peerless prophet of Israel, was but a boy when his mother entrusted him to the tutorage of the high priest, Eli, at the tabernacle in Shiloh. Eli's two sons were notorious, and he had no control over them whatsoever. They met a horrible death near the altar of God, when consuming flames burst forth upon them, ending their sorry lives.

Oddly enough, years later Samuel himself had two unruly sons whose behavior was so deplorable that Israel refused to permit either one of them to receive the mantle of leadership from their father. How intriguing that Samuel would end up with essentially the same family problems of his surrogate father, old Eli. Like father; like son?

But there's more. Despite being a man after God's own heart, David the great warrior king of Israel, fell into a lustful affair with Bathsheba and then murdered her husband to cover it up. His repentance is legendary, as is the Lord's forgiveness. Nevertheless, his choices unleashed trouble for his linage. "The sword shall never depart from your house," the prophet Nathan told him, and a review of the following years proved the saying was true.[3]

Solomon, the love child of David and Bathsheba, was a man so emotionally insecure it took *thousands* of women to satisfy him. And even that still wasn't enough! Solomon ran an epic marathon of madness, searching out "everything under the sun" to excessive measures. Surely, that can be traced somewhat to David's failures as a dad. Like father; like son.

The stories go on and on, from one generation to the next; from one people to the next; from one family to the next. It would seem that in each of these scenarios the fathers, now sobered with age, could say in unison, *"Dear God, son, I built that prison."*

The sins of the fathers are indeed visited upon their children to the third and fourth generation; over and over again. And for the record, the rest of that oft quoted passage from the Old Testament goes on to say that, while the father's sins impact three to four generations of those who hate God, He shows mercy unto *thousands* of them who love Him and keep His commandments.[4]

You can stop the cycle of bondage in your family history, and unleash a powerful surge of blessings for generations to come! How? By answering the call God has upon your life. And I am writing to help you do just that.

Of the many grand declarations in scripture, few are more marvelous than this:

"If any man be in Christ, he is a new creation; old things have passed away; behold, all things have become new" (2 Co. 5:17).

It is true. God can change *any* life and alter the course of history by so doing. "Before I shaped you in the womb, I knew all about you," God said to Jeremiah. "Before you saw the light of day, I had holy plans for you."[5]

Do you suppose that God might have also known all about *you* before you were born? Of course He did! And in the same way He had plans for Jeremiah, He also has plans for you.

> *"I know the plans I have for you,"* declares the LORD, *"plans to prosper you and not to harm you, plans to give you hope and a future."*
> (Jeremiah 29:11).

This applies to you, your children, and to your children's children – for a *thousand* generations!

"Before you saw the light of day, I had holy plans for you."

Before I move on to discuss how we can be released from the prisons our fathers have built and step into the cycle of God's blessings, there was one more thing that struck me about dad's answer that night in his den.

It wasn't just that I was in the very prison where he had welded the bars, but that while there I had been enrolled in the vocational program where they teach you a trade you can use once you are released. You want to take a guess at which class they put me in?

Yep, *welding*.

We'll talk about this some more a little bit later on; but first, let me introduce you to a few monsters.

Chapter Four
A Monster Named Sally

Nobody explained to me what was actually happening as we drove those five hours along Interstate 20 from Midland, Texas to Dallas – I just knew *something* was not right. There was nervous tension in the air, despite the occasional laughter sprinkled in between rounds of "I Spy" and other assorted road games that keeps kids from asking, "Are we there yet?"

We arrived at what they called THE RECEIVING HOME in the hot Texas summer of '57. Mom and her sister-in-law, Aunt Tootie, somehow managed to keep their composure as they handed us over to Sally Polk, the director of the home; a large, middle-aged lady with a foul and intemperate disposition.

THE RECEIVING HOME was the place kids went before being admitted onto the larger campus of BUCKNER ORPHAN'S HOME. The idea was to inoculate us from any germs and contaminants we might be carrying. It was also a place of indoctrination into how we were expected to behave once there.

We watched from the window as the car drove away, following with our eyes until it faded out of sight. My brother Jere, almost two years older than me, and my sister Valerie, five years older, both knew what was going on. I did not.

Mom was leaving us there, and she would *not* be coming back. Valerie and Jere wept uncontrollably as they watched mom drive away. Just three months shy of seven years old, I was clueless and confused – a condition that would soon change. For old Sally Polk was a force to be reckoned with – a massive woman, weighing about 300 pounds. She had weird eyes that operated independent of each other, like that lizard you see on National Geographic; so you never knew exactly where Sally was looking.

Mom was leaving us there, and she would *not* be coming back.

And she didn't walk, as much as she waddled. Shifting her enormous weight from one foot to the other and landing with such force that the floor would vibrate, and the water in your glass would ripple. You know, like T-Rex in Jurassic Park. It didn't take long for us all to learn that when you heard that sound and saw those ripples, *the Monster* was on her way.

One evening at dinnertime, we were seated around the table with about five other kids who had also been left there. The boy to my right, Rodney, became sick and threw up into his plate and on the table. What happened next was shocking beyond belief – the monster, filled with indignation at his lack of self-control, forced him to eat his own vomit!

I was terrified. Call it self-preservation instinct, or whatever, but at that moment something inside me disconnected from the scene and I went "invisible." Staring silently and motionless into my plate, I somehow managed to get through the meal and then vanished into my room, where I cried myself to sleep. That would be the first of many horrific and inhumane experiences that would unfold over the following years.

A week later we were moved onto the Buckner campus; a large sprawling complex of dormitories, schools, service buildings, and a massive church located near the center of the campus.

The huge sanctuary, large enough to hold over a thousand people, was overwhelming to me when I first entered it. Painted on the front walls in large, golden letters were the words, "BE STILL AND KNOW THAT I AM GOD" (Psalm 46:10), and "THE LORD IS IN HIS HOLY TEMPLE; LET ALL THE EARTH KEEP SILENCE BEFORE HIM" (Habakkuk 2:20).

To a young boy unfamiliar with the church world the message was clear, *"Be still and be quiet!"*

As an adult I've often wondered if that was the reason the adults had put those specific verses on the walls in the first place; you know, kind of a subliminal attempt to maintain control over unwanted and unruly kids. Whatever the reason, it had an effect upon me: I grew *fearful* of God.

In fact, the first of many beatings I received at the orphanage was for misbehaving during a church service. Some kid farted and I giggled. Evidently, God didn't think that was funny. As it turned out there were *lots* of things He didn't think were funny, and the house parents made it their mission to educate me in such matters. And their methods of education were frightening - and *scandalous*.

They called it the *belt line*, and the way it worked was like this. All the boys in the orphanage dormitory took part in the ordeal by standing along the hallway on both sides, with their leather belts in hand. One lone boy, guilty of who knows what, had to take off his shirt and pull his pants down about his ankles - this was so that he couldn't run, nor even walk too fast. They wanted this to take some time.

Clad only in underwear, the boy then had to make his way down the hall, with every other boy striking him as hard and as often as possible with their belts, as he passed

29

within their reach. Some of the boys were vicious and perverse, striking with cruel intention at parts of the body that would hurt the most. If you covered your face, they would hit at your private parts. If you tried to shield that part of your body, they would strike about your face – laughing hysterically and screaming like jackals.

Pity the boy who stumbled and fell, for there was no limit to how many blows could be landed while he was down. I had to walk the infamous belt line *twice*.

There were also many other equally inventive measures of punishment used to secure unflinching obedience. Once I was forced to bend over a toilet and swallow spoonfuls of dry Epson Salt until I vomited; this was to clean my mouth out for saying dirty words. You can imagine the string of words I let loose after that ordeal was done!

On some occasions boys were required to spank themselves in front of the other kids. If the others didn't think the spankings were hard enough, they each then got to take their turn at him with the paddle. Needless to say, this place was anything but loving and nurturing. It was, in a word, terrifying.

The place held about 1200 kids. Managing them was the primary concern of the approximately 200 staff members. We were placed in dormitories according to our age and gender. I was assigned to a dorm that held about forty other 7-9 year old boys. Maybe once a week I would see my brother, Jere, at "the corner" - a place located just in front of the huge church. And perhaps three times a month I would see Valerie, my sister.

Even though we were each in the same situation, we were separated from one another and lost that bond that holds families together. Our lives would never be the same. Even to this day there yet remains a strange disconnection between us, though we are siblings. To make matters worse, our two older brothers, Frank and Randy, were in yet another Children's Home miles away in West Texas. All in all it was a real bad deal, and none of us could do anything about it.

Life in my dorm was like a scene from the Lost Boys in Peter Pan. And somehow you had to figure out how to survive - act a certain way, fly beneath the radar, avoid any trouble - because Sally Polk was not the only monster in all this madness. There were others.

"Barrel-Butt" Barnes was what we called her behind her back, because her rear was disproportionately large for her frame. And when she walked, her backside looked like two pigs fighting under a blanket. She was a fierce and miserable woman, who took seriously her charge of keeping young boys in line.

She even went so far as to sit in a folding chair watching us take showers; just to make sure there would be no horsing around in there. Is it only me, or does that strike you as just a little too weird? I mean, just at the time when young boys are discovering they have wing-wangs, there's this brooding woman watching them take showers. Now that's just not right anyway you look at it.

The other woman, Miss Walker, had an ominous presence about her that seemed ready to explode at any moment. We called her Old Battle-Ax. Remember the Queen from Alice in Wonderland? The slightest infraction would result in her royal decree, *"Off with her head!"* That was what you expected from Old Battle-Ax at any moment. My first brush with her fire came quite unexpectedly one day.

The Bible was used, not so much as a Good Book filled with the hope of salvation and better things to come, but more as a weapon to insure control, discipline and order.

On one occasion Pastor Powell, a Baptist minister who lived on campus and preached each Sunday in the large church, issued a challenge from the pulpit. "We need to read the Bible more," he said, "and so I challenge each of you to start in Genesis first thing Monday morning, and see how far you can get by next Sunday."

So I did it. I took a Gideon Bible and started reading, "In the beginning God created the heavens and the earth. And the earth was without form, and void; and darkness was upon the face of the deep. And the Spirit of God moved upon the face of the waters. And God said, Let there be light: and there was light."

I was hooked! I kept reading and came to the serpent in the garden, and the guilty pair being expelled into the outlands. And I read about Methuselah, the oldest man who ever lived; and Noah's Ark; and Father Abraham, and the Promised Land. Then I read about Joseph, a young dreamer who was placed in a pit and then sold into slavery by his brothers. I read about how he went through awful things until he was exalted by God to become a ruler in Egypt.

"You meant it for evil, but God meant it for good."

And then I read these words, spoken by Joseph to his erring kin, *"You meant it for evil, but God meant it for good."* Despite his awful ordeal, it had all worked out good in the end. Somehow my young heart identified with Joseph, and I dared to think that things would work out for me, too.

By Thursday of that week I had finished reading the book of Genesis, and I went to Miss Walker and told her with triumphant exuberance, "Miss Walker, I read the whole book of Genesis!" I was hoping she would be impressed with me and give me that proverbial pat on the head every boy longs to receive from anybody – but especially from his his dad.

Instead she turned toward me with a fiery scowl on her face and snapped, "You little liar! You did no such thing. *Nobody* could read Genesis in one week."

Right then I knew two things for sure. One, I did too read it. And, two, she did *not*. I also knew that I could never go to her again with anything that mattered. Over the following years I learned that very few of the adults working there could be counted on when it really mattered. I was lost in a crowd of unwanted kids, and I was alone.

Yet, the Lord was with me - even though I didn't know it at the time. "When my father and my mother forsake me," the Psalmist wrote, "then the LORD will take me up!" (Psalm 27:10). This scripture holds great promise for countless abandoned children in today's disordered world. Perhaps you are one of them. God is the Father of the fatherless, and His name is on the line each time a child is forsaken by his or her parents.

The word *forsake* means, "to loosen and let go; to leave exposed and thereby permit *anything* to happen." It is the ultimate act of parental irresponsibility. But the Lord does not stand by indifferently when parents drop the ball. He *takes up* the discarded kids, one and all. To "take up" means "to gather an individual into a company of others; to collect (as something of great value), and to harvest as something of great purpose."

Did you know that you matter that much to God? He sees you as someone of great value, and views your life as one having great purpose. Perhaps right now you are unable to see that, or even believe it – but it is true.

The Prayers of Children

About a year into my stay at the Orphanage, two boys ran away from our dormitory and the place was filled with alarm and anxiety. Old Battle-Ax and Barrel Butt Barnes paced about wringing their hands, fearing the worst. The State Troopers were called and a search was started to find those two little guys, who were no more than nine years old.

It took three days to locate them walking along the Interstate, headed for parts unknown. The Troopers brought them safely back and delivered them into the waiting arms of Miss Walker, who drew them tightly into her big bosom and acted for a minute like a real mother. She thanked the Troopers and held the boys tightly as the officers drove away.

And then all hell broke loose. Those little guys got the living daylights beat out of them. Miss Walker laid into them with her *paddle* – a baseball bat sawn long ways into a flat board and wrapped with duct tape to insure it wouldn't break. Then, holes were drilled through the board which caused blisters on the skin once the blow was landed.

To a dorm filled with terrified boys, it sounded like she hit fifty homeruns that night. The rage in her voice, the sound of that board striking those boys, and their screams echoed through our dorm – aided by the cement floors and plaster walls. I have never forgotten that night. It was on that night I prayed my first prayer ever to a God I did not know, but greatly feared.

By this time I had at least figured out that God ran the orphanage. At least that's the impression given to us by the adults who would brandish the Bible like the old Southern landowners would use a whip.

That night I wanted *this* God to know that from then on I was going to be a good little boy. *"Dear God,"* I said, pulling the bed covers up about my chin like a security blanket, *"I promise I will never run away."* Remember, I was only seven years old at the time.

Now, as an adult looking back all those years ago, I realize God was not behind all this nonsense. "When I was a child I spoke as a child, I understood as a child, I thought as a child; but when I became a man, I put away childish things."[6]

Even then, though I could not hear His voice, God was saying, *"Oh, child; this is not the way I am. And one day you will know Me, and we will walk as friends."*

Chapter Five
The God Who Speaks

The years passed and I kept a low profile, avoiding trouble whenever possible. With increasing exposure to the world that existed beyond the fence, I began to question the things taking place inside the orphanage. There comes a point in a boy's life where he begins to see through the senseless behavior of adults who are still trying to figure things out for themselves.

For me that happened when I was fourteen. That's when two friends and I decided to run away.

We carefully made our plans and preparations. After stocking up with candy bars and potato chips from the campus commissary and sketching out a make-shift map of our route of escape, we were ready.

Finally the day came. We snuck out of the dorm about 2am, wearing camouflage military jackets that had been donated to the orphanage by the Army Surplus Store, and wiping shoe polish on our faces so the moon wouldn't give us away. Then with serpentine moves we made our way to the fence that stood between us and The Great Beyond.

The fence was no challenge; it was a standard four-foot chain link. We conquered it with one leap. Next was the highway, and the field on the other side, and off in the distance - the Woods. If we could make it to the darkened Woods before the German Shepherds were unleashed, we would be free! (Bear with me here, I was only fourteen and highly imaginative). And it will help if while you are reading this, you play the theme music for "Mission Impossible" in your head.

Disobedience can be really fun sometimes, and that night was one of those times. We were breaking the rules and getting away with it. Our hearts raced with adrenaline and a wild youthful sense of adventure.

Halfway across the field, with the Woods beckoning us onward, we could detect no stir on the campus. No alarm sounded; no lights turned on. They didn't even know we were gone. We were but a few hundred yards from disappearing into the Woods when something happened that I was not prepared for.

The voice of the Lord spoke to me out of the silence, stopping me in my tracks. No, it was not audible; but it was unmistakable.

"You promised."

That's all He said, but it was enough. I was stunned. Seven years had passed since the night I made that promise as a frightened child. Now, standing in the middle of a plowed field, the Lord reminded me of it.

My first thought was, *"I can't believe that You would bring that up at a time like this!"* I didn't know what to do. I mean, why didn't He say something during the week we were making our plans? Why didn't He stop me before I put the shoe polish on my face - that would've been thoughtful of Him. Why wait until I'm in the middle of the field, so close to freedom?

My two friends, unaware of what was happening, continued running into the darkness of the night while I stood there wrestling with a choice I did not want to make. I looked back at the orphanage, and then turned to see my two buddies fading into the night. What was I to do? Which way would I go?

I made my choice. "But You know what it's like there," I whispered to God, and then said, "I'm sorry, but I can't go back." Regrettably, I broke my childhood promise to God that night. It was a stupid choice, and, as I mentioned earlier - even then I was following in my father's erring footsteps.

I've often wondered what would have happened had I kept my promise to God that night, turned around and gone back - how different might things have been for me. I'm certain I would be following the Lord today, as I am now. He was obviously calling me to that end. But surely the road would have been, shall we say, less complicated.

Still, that night in the field was for me a defining moment, for it was the first time I ever heard God's voice. And that's not something you forget. And thankfully, even though I turned away, it would not be the last.

There are many ways in which the still, small voice of God can be heard.

As I mentioned earlier, there was the occasion when He said, "All things work together for good, for those who love God and are called according to His purpose." It was a timely word that buoyed my spirit with faith to face the ordeal of prison, which loomed large before me.

And then, just days before I was released from prison He had spoken to me again, saying, "Go home to your friends and tell them what great things the Lord has done."

You may have noticed that God often speaks to me through Bible verses. Yes, God does speak to us through the Bible, but He also speaks in many other ways, each one in keeping with what the Scriptures teach.

He speaks to us in parables, and in dreams and visions; in random thoughts and incidental ways. He also speaks in coincidental ways. He speaks in the quiet moments of contemplative observations, as well as in the midst of thunderous upheavals and great heartbreaks. There are many ways in which the still, small voice of God can be heard by men and women, boys and girls.

Perhaps He is speaking to you even now.

One thing I have learned through all of this is that God truly cares about us. He wants us to know Him personally, and to enjoy life as we walk with Him each day. There is no question in my mind that the personal friendship, which began to develop between Jesus and me while I was in prison, surely carried me forward with hope and great expectations once I was released.

In fact, a few months after my release from prison I was reading the Bible and came upon yet another one of those passages that seemed to leap from the page into my heart. It became not only the summary of my testimony, but somewhat of a prophecy for the following years of my life as I continued walking with Jesus.

> *"I waited patiently for the LORD, and He inclined to me, and heard my cry. He brought me up also out of a horrible pit, out of the miry clay; He set my feet upon a rock, and established my goings. He has put a new song in my mouth - a song of praise to our God. Many will see, and fear, and will trust in the LORD"* (Psalm 40:1-3).

It was as if I had written those words myself. I *had* cried unto the Lord from the depths of a horrible pit, and He *had* heard me and lifted me up; placed me on a rock, and established my goings. He *had* filled my mouth with song. But the last phrase is what stirred my imagination: *"Many will see, and fear, and will trust in the Lord"*

Somehow those words seemed to foretell a brighter future than I could have ever imagined for myself. Inasmuch as the first part of the verse fit so well to my own story, then (I reasoned) the remainder of the verse would somehow be true also.

And now, all these years later, I can testify that the Lord has indeed done what He said He would do. He has graciously given me the extraordinary privilege of telling my story to hundreds of thousands of people - not only in the US, but also abroad. Truly, *many* have seen, and have stood in awe of God, placing their trust in Him as they have listened to my story of the great things the Lord has done.

To me, it is a wondrous thing by itself that the Lord actually did this. But *how* He did it is even more remarkable to tell.

Promise Keepers

"I want you to be chaplain for the University of Colorado Football Team," Coach Bill McCartney said to me one day, in a way that let me know it really wasn't open for discussion.

Football coaches are like that. I once heard Tom Landry say, "A coach is a man who makes men do what they don't want to do, so that they can become everything they always wanted to be." That's the way it was with Coach McCartney. He wanted me to be the team chaplain - and that was that.

"What do you want me to do?" I asked, "Motivate them?"

"Of course not," he answered, "that's *my* job."

"Well, then what exactly do you want me to do?" I replied, not really sure what he was thinking.

"I want you to do what you do," he said, "only *quicker!*"

So I *was* a long-winded preacher. One church member even told me, "Pastor, your sermons are like the grace of God - beyond understanding, and without end!"

And even my own son, David, when he was serving as Youth Pastor, went into the men's bathroom and stuck a post-it note on the air-powered hand dryer. The note read, "Push here for a message from Pastor James." Bless you, my son.

So Mac wanted me to do what I was good at doing, only *quicker.* And he had good reasons. When you are speaking to football players on Game Day, you really don't have a lot of time to preach three-point sermons that end with poems. And, as I discovered my first day, jokes usually do not go over very well, for these guys are *not* in a laughing mood. They've been working up all week long to unleash the full force of their physical fury against their opponents - and you're standing in front of them clowning around? I don't think so.

In just a few short weeks I learned that being a stand-up guy and speaking truth straight to their hearts was the only thing these brutes would respect. So that was the approach I took. Evidently it was the right approach; I was a part of the CU football program for ten years.

But the Lord was up to something that neither I, nor Bill McCartney, would have ever imagined. The very fact that He even brought the two of us together was out of the ordinary.

Never were there two more unlikely friends than Bill and me. He was a hard-nosed football coach; a no nonsense disciplinarian; a dyed-in-the-wool, blue-collared Michigan Catholic. And me, I was an ex-con, ex-hippie, non-jock,

Bible-toting charismatic, who wrote poetry and looked for animal formations in the clouds.

He a Spartan; me a Thespian. He a warrior; me an orator. He a man of action; me a dreamer. He a leader of men; me a self-conscious, insecure guy still sorting out what it was like growing up without a dad...or a mom.

And the Lord looked down upon the sons of men, and said, "Yes, I think I will use those two guys to do something unbelievable."

But, lest you think that we considered ourselves to be somewhat exceptional, remember this - *"God uses the foolish to confound the wise."*[7] We were fools, and still are to this day; that was our only qualification.

It began in the summer of '89. I had a dream in which I saw the Colorado football team huddled together under a dark cloud. Then, as though an invisible hand pushed it to the side, the cloud removed from the team and they were huddled in the open sunlight. A rainbow arced from the cloud into the huddle of players, whose black jerseys and gold helmets gave the appearance of a pot of gold at the end of the rainbow. That's what I saw.

And then I heard a voice say, "This will be their golden season," and as I lifted my eyes to see who was speaking I awakened from my dream. It was about 3am. I lay there and thought about it for a while.

I had the strongest sense that God was showing me that He was going to bless the team in an obvious way. Even the rainbow suggested that God would fulfill promises He had made to Mac; at least that's what I surmised from it all.

Later that day, August 22, 1989, I told this dream to Coach during practice. I remember the date specifically, because it was his birthday. "Here's a birthday present from the Lord," I said in charismatic flair.

Two weeks later we faced our first opponents for the season - the Texas Longhorns. During breakfast on Game Day I told Mac that I was praying for him, and had asked God to give him a sign. "I'm praying that you beat Texas big time," I said, "so you will know this is going to be a *Golden Season.*"

Mac looked me in the eye, set his eating utensils down beside his plate, folded his hands below his chin, and said, *"You really know nothing about college football, do you?"*

"No," I frankly admitted, "but I *do* know the Lord. And I also know that He is going to do something special this season - that's all I'm saying."

Colorado *did* beat Texas that day with a commanding victory, but what we found more astounding were the headlines the following morning in the Rocky Mountain News - "Buffs Have a Golden Season Debut!"[8]

We were aware that something bigger than football was going on here.

From that moment forward we were aware that something bigger than football was going on here. We went undefeated that year, despite losing our senior quarterback Sal Aunese to cancer. However, Notre Dame defeated us in the Orange Bowl. It was for the National Championship, and we came up short.

Exactly one year later, after a nail-biting season which included the infamous fifth-down controversy in Missouri, we faced Notre Dame once again in the Orange Bowl, for the National Championship - and this time we won. And there was no doubt in our minds that this victory was not by our merits alone.

On the plane ride home Mac told me his thoughts about what he saw the Lord doing in all of this. He felt strongly that God was blessing him with success as a coach in order to use that platform to reach men all across America with a call to become men of integrity – *Promise Keepers.*

Men and sports go together like steak and potatoes. God loves men and will reach out to them in ways they can understand. How interesting, then, that God raised up a football coach to call men together in such numbers that it boggles the mind even to this day.

We held our first meeting in Boulder with about seventy guys, and Coach Mac cast the vision of filling the football stadium with men who were unashamed of Jesus; men who would keep their promises to the Lord, to their wives and families, and to others. We each agreed to pray for one year and then meet again in Boulder to see what the Lord would do.

The year passed quickly and when we gathered in the Coors Event Center on the CU campus, more than four thousand men showed up. Word of mouth had created a grass-roots movement.

One year later we met again – this time at Folsom Field, home to the Colorado Buffaloes. More than 22,000 men came. One year later, 54,000 men gathered in Boulder for a two-day stadium conference.

Promise Keepers had tapped into a great hunger in the hearts of men all across the nation, and those large numbers were just the tip of the iceberg.

The following year PK convened six stadium events, attended by over 350,000 men. The year after that fourteen stadiums filled with over 700,000 guys. Each year the numbers swelled into the hundreds of thousands, as PK continued holding multiple events in stadiums all across America. It was my great honor to be a part of the speaking team for many of those events

Perhaps you can now appreciate how astonished I was personally, when, on October 4, 1997, I stood at the podium in Washington, DC, delivering the Gospel Message to over 1.4 million men who were gathered for a *Promise Keepers* event called STAND IN THE GAP - the single largest Christian gathering of men in history.

"Many will see, and fear, and will trust in the Lord." That was a promise the Lord had made to me all those years back when, as a young man fresh out of prison and taking my first awkward steps in ministry, I dared to believe He would use me.

He will use you too. "For the eyes of the Lord run to and fro throughout the whole earth, to show Himself strong on behalf of those whose heart is loyal to Him" (2 Chronicles 16:9, NKJV). Open your heart to the Lord and listen for His voice; believe Him when He speaks, and do what He says to do.

Your life will never be the same - *I promise.*

Lord of the Rings

I have a championship ring. Actually, I have two. One is the Big Eight Conference Championship ring (now the Big Twelve). The other is the 1991 National Championship ring. In the collegiate world of football it's a pretty big deal to win both. So you can imagine the excitement we all felt at Colorado when it happened. And although I was only the Chaplain, I was included when the rings were handed out. They even have my name on them. Wow.

But there's just one problem. The rings do not fit. And I don't understand why. I was measured before the rings were made, and was eager to put them on when they arrived. But, no, they were both too small. Dang!

I stood there in my room trying to figure out a way to make them fit me, but nothing I did worked. After spitting on my finger I was able to force the ring over my knuckle. But then my finger swelled up like a hot dog. I was barely able to get the ring off before it was too late.

Do you know what a drag it is to have two Championship rings that you can't wear? I remember muttering under my breath a half-hearted complaint to the Lord about this. "They're too small," I said. And then in one of those moments that you never forget the Lord spoke to my heart, "That's right. They *are* too small. I have called you to something bigger than football games and championship rings."

> **"Go home to your friends, and tell them the great things the Lord has done."**

As a chaplain I watched a football team devote themselves with Spartan-like dedication to a cause that ultimately, on the Grand Stage of life, is short-lived and soon forgotten by all but those who paid the price to win it. My question is this: if these guys would pay so dearly for that which means so little, what in the world is holding us back from giving our all for Christ?

In the words of Paul, "They do it to obtain a corruptible crown, but we an incorruptible" (1 Corinthians 9:25). Shouldn't our dedication exceed theirs to the same degree that our prize excels theirs? Indeed, it should!

Hearkening back over the years I cannot wander far from the words the Lord spoke to me shortly before my release from the prison my father built - *"Go home to your friends and tell them the great things the Lord has done."*

So that's what I'm doing. And as I do so, I cannot help but note the irony that as a runaway teen I broke a promise to God, which led me down a dark path that nearly destroyed me. And yet, despite it all, I ended up helping Bill McCartney start a movement called *Promise Keepers*.

Hmmm. I wonder if the Lord knew that all along.

There is one more part of my story that is the hardest of all for me to tell, for it involves the deepest wound and greatest pain I have ever experienced. But, I must tell you about it because it shows how the Lord can rescue us from the brink of disaster by the truth of His Word and the nearness of His presence.

It also shows the power of forgiveness and the freedom that comes when we trust the Lord – even in our darkest moments.

Chapter Six
On the Brink of Disaster

Never in a million years would I have believed that such a thing could ever happen. But it did. And I would not wish it upon my worst enemy. It would've been unbearable in any situation, but what made this thing so diabolically awful is that it happened in *the Church*.

The pastor sexually violated my wife.

In a place that was supposed to be a sanctuary from the world, a refuge from all that is dark and wicked, an evil thing was done. And by a man who was supposed to be a shepherd of the flock, a defender of the weak, and a champion of truth.

This violation of everything we hold dearest pushed me to the brink of disaster. I was a man with *murder* on my mind. I had the motive, the means, and the opportunity. And I would have surely fallen into the abyss had not the Lord intervened.

> ### I was a man with *murder* on my mind.

Six years earlier, in 1974, Belinda and I accepted an invitation to join a local church staff. We arrived with much excitement, eager to serve faithfully and were ready to make a difference. I had no reason to suspect that anything was wrong. However, it didn't take long for the glow of this new frontier to fade away. Soon there was a gloom that hung over everything like fog on a cold September morning.

The pastor, who shall remain unnamed for the sake of others who are innocent, was a charismatic man. He was very gifted and quite charming. Yet he was also deeply miserable; a man filled with the torment of lifelong disapproval and driven by anger to prove that others were wrong for rejecting him. Somehow he had mastered the art of masking his inner demons. He projected an outward confidence that drew a sizeable following.

As for me, I was naïve and eager to please, trusting and compliant to a fault. Having grown up without a father, I found this man to be quite fascinating. I was clueless of just how dark and dreadful things really were beneath the shining surface of this fallen man's charismatic world.

He was an independent man of strong opinions and few friends. He had been the worship leader at a prominent Baptist church in Denver, but an encounter with the Holy Spirit ended all that. Rejected from the fold, he became a maverick, leading a band of disenchanted Baptists into what was called "the deeper life."

As his associate pastor I did my best for six years to help build up the congregation and grow the church. But despite our youthful enthusiasm and unflagging zeal, we nevertheless experienced what is often referred to as a "back-door revival" – more people *leaving* the church than coming. Unable to put their finger on exactly what was wrong, and chastised by the man of God anytime they questioned his leadership, these battle-worn souls found no reprieve except in leaving the church.

And those who left were always blasted with a few of the pastor's favorite Bible texts. "Touch not God's anointed!"[9] he would say, to insure his standing with those who remained. As for those who departed – "They went out from us for they were not of us; for had they been, they would have remained!"[10] The angry pastor would then warn the dwindling congregation to "have nothing to do with those who cause division."[11] And though I am ashamed to admit it, I stood by his side and championed his cause not knowing any better at the time.

The church could no longer afford to pay salaries. I took a job in an auto paint and body shop – which was owned by the pastor. He didn't pay me very much, because we were living in the house owned by the church. It was while I was working in his shop that he started making his "pastoral visits" to my house.

The Lord watched from Heaven, and the storm clouds started gathering.

Belinda and I were struggling. I was more focused on ministry than on her, and my neglect left an opening for his smooth words and subtle ways. It began with a kiss and a touch. Belinda was shocked and, yes, intimidated. "If you tell anyone about this," he told her, "I will deny it. And who do you think they will believe – you, or me?"

The trap was set. Her silence gave him unrestricted access to press the matter further, and he seized the opportunity. He repeated his visits and took advantage of my wife for several months. The Lord watched from heaven, and the storm clouds started gathering. "Be sure your sins will find you out,"[12] the Bible warns. And this man's sins were soon discovered.

The Visit of a Friend

Bob Hensley, a friend who had done much to help me take my first steps as a follower of Jesus in the months after my release from prison, came to visit us in our church. It had been about eight years since we had last seen him, and we were thrilled to welcome a friendly face into our beleaguered world.

Bob arrived on a Thursday night and we visited late into the evening. We recalled our earlier days together in Grand Prairie, Texas, when God moved mightily in a coffee house ministry called The True Vine. We remembered fondly the many times and ways in which the Lord had touched and changed so many lives in those days.

Our conversation shifted to the present, and there wasn't much to say.

"We're hanging in there," I said. "You know, trusting God for a breakthrough." It sounded like the right thing to say, but it was weak, especially in contrast with the vibrant ministry we had been discussing.

I went to work the next morning and Bob went to have a meeting with our pastor. He knew nothing of what was going on. But, as a friend, he could tell we were unhappy. He hoped that spending time with the pastor would help turn things around for us. He was right, it did. But not in ways he ever imagined.

I got home from work about 6pm. Belinda was there, but not Bob. "Heard anything from Bob?" I asked.

"Not a word," she said.

"Well, I wonder where he is," I mused aloud.

The evening drew on into the night with no news from Bob. About midnight, we saw the headlights of Bob's car pull into the driveway. I got out of bed to meet him. When he walked in the door the look on his face was alarming. He was drained of all energy and pale with grave concern.

"I just spent the past several hours with a demon!" he said.

Of course, that statement set me off and I began to defend the man of God, my pastor. Bob politely stopped me in my tracks and for the next three hours patiently dismantled my arguments point by point.

Suddenly it hit me like a ton of bricks. "Oh my God," I said out loud. "What have I gotten us into?" The blinders were off. I now saw in the face of my friend what I could not see in the façade of my pastor.

"Oh my God," I said out loud. "What have I gotten us into?"

I still knew nothing of the sexual violations against Belinda. The predator pastor had worked her over with such guilt and shame that she had become convinced nobody would ever believe her if she said anything about it – including me.

All I knew at the time was that the pastor was wrong in so many ways. I had to talk to him face to face as a friend. I thought he would surely listen to me; after all, I had stood faithfully by his side through everything that had happened up to this point. Surely he would hear what I had to say to him. I could not have been more mistaken.

Bob left the next morning, which was Saturday. I called the pastor to let him know I was coming over to talk with him. I knew that facing this man would be a defining moment.

Though I appealed to him to get some help from other pastors who could counsel him in his personal life as well as his pastoral role, he blew up. I was summarily dismissed as nothing more than another misguided soul who had turned away from the Truth.

In that single moment I lost my home, my church, my job, and my friends. But I did not lose my faith.

I left the pastor and went home to Belinda. We embraced sitting on the sofa and cried together for over an hour. Later, I called a pastor friend in a neighboring city and told him about our predicament. His church rallied to our aid and helped us find another home we could use for a while. They also helped me find work in another auto paint and body shop.

The Moment of Truth

We moved away from the old church and started a slow healing process with a new circle of friends. After a couple of months it seemed that the dark season was now far behind us. But, in fact, I was quickly approaching the brink of disaster – and didn't even know it.

One evening, after a long, grinding day's work, I arrived home dog-tired and covered with grime from the paint and body shop. Belinda met me at the door with a look on her face that sent shivers up my spine. Something was wrong….. *bad* wrong.

"Honey," she said in a quivering voice, "there is something I have to tell you."

I knew it was not going to be anything I wanted to hear, but she was determined; this was something she *had* to do. I sat down and gave her my full attention. What she said next crumbled me to the floor.

"When we were at the old church, the pastor came to our house while you were at work and sexually molested me."

Words cannot adequately tell the depths of anguish and rage I felt over the next few hours. I fell to the floor in complete surrender to a pain far too overwhelming for me to handle. I sobbed in great heaves that shook my body. A sound, like a train in a mountain tunnel, rose from deep inside my soul. I wailed in such heartbreak and anger that it left me completely spent. Betrayal can be one of the most devastating experiences anyone ever faces in life.

During this emotional ordeal I kept seeing this pastor's face pass before my mind. I recalled the many times he had smugly dismissed others as being deceived, including me. The more I saw his face, the angrier I became.

Somewhere in the vortex of those swirling thoughts, murder entered my mind. I left the house and rode my motorcycle up to Lookout Mountain, and started thinking seriously about how I could put an end to this man's miserable life. And I meant to do it that night.

Betrayal can be one of the most devastating experiences one ever faces in life.

I went so far as to devise a plan whereby I could conceivably pull it off without being caught. And, if I did get caught, it wouldn't matter - I felt I had nothing left worth living for now anyway. My mind was set; I was going to go get my gun, drive to his home and kill him. But the Lord stepped in and brought me back from the brink of disaster.

"James," He said, "I know that this man has sinned against you and that you feel it would be unjust of Me to ask you to forgive him" That was exactly how I felt. The Lord continued, "There is a time when it is right in My eyes for you *not* to forgive another."

I was "all ears" for I thought this surely was such a time. The Lord seemed to pause as if to ensure that He had my full attention, then He delivered the knockout blow. "You are right to withhold forgiveness from another whenever they sin against you *more* than you have sinned against Me!"

When Jesus Tells a Story...

It is sometimes difficult to explain how the Lord speaks, for His ways are not our ways. He doesn't talk in sentences; He speaks in flashes of light that fill our hearts with pictures, and each picture is worth a thousand words. What we experience in an instant, may take us several minutes to explain to others.

In that instant I remembered the story Jesus told about the Unmerciful Servant, and I knew He was speaking to me. Opening my Bible I read the following words:

"Then Peter came to Him and said, 'Lord, how often shall my brother sin against me, and I forgive him? Up to seven times?' Jesus said to him, 'I do not say to you, up to seven times, but up to seventy times seven.'" (Matthew 18:21,22)

That verse by itself stopped me in my tracks. "You mean I'm just supposed to forgive this guy like nothing happened?" I said. "What he did was wrong! And waving it off like it doesn't matter *cannot* be right!"

I continued reading.

"Therefore the kingdom of heaven is like a certain king who wanted to settle accounts with his servants. And when he had begun to settle accounts, one was brought to him who owed him ten thousand talents. But as he was not able to pay, his master commanded that he be sold, with his wife and children and all that he had, and that payment be made. The servant therefore fell down before him, saying, 'Master, have patience with me, and I will pay you all.'

"Then the master of that servant was moved with compassion, released him, and forgave him the debt. But that servant went out and found one of his fellow servants who owed him a hundred talents; and he laid hands on him and took him by the throat, saying, 'Pay me what you owe!' So his fellow servant fell down at his feet and begged him, saying, 'Have patience with me, and I will pay you all.' And he would not, but went and threw him into prison till he should pay the debt.

"So when his fellow servants saw what had been done, they were very grieved, and came and told their master all that had been done. Then his master, after he had called him, said to him, 'You wicked servant! I forgave you all that debt because you begged me. Should you not also have had compassion on your fellow servant, just as I had pity on you?'

"And his master was angry, and delivered him to the torturers until he should pay all that was due to him. So My heavenly Father also will do to you if each of you, from his heart, does not forgive his brother his trespasses." (Matthew 18:21-35)

I gasped as these words pierced my heart. Yes, this pastor had sinned against me greatly. But it was *nothing* compared to how much I had sinned against the Lord. And seeing how the Lord had forgiven me my great debt, how could I possibly withhold forgiveness from this man?

I broke before the Lord and admitted that such a thing could never be, crying out, "I forgive him, Lord; I forgive him!" The Holy Spirit flooded my heart and released me from the grip of my own anger. I was free from the rage over what this man had done to us!

I learned two very valuable lessons that night. First, forgiveness is a matter of *focus.* As long as you look at what others have done against you it will be virtually impossible to forgive them. But, when you keep your eyes upon all the Lord has forgiven *you* - the great debt you owed and could not pay - it becomes remarkably easy to release them into the Lord's hand.

Secondly, and this is very important for victims to understand, forgiveness does not mean that what the person did against you is now alright, or that they are going to "get away with it." Rather, it is your acknowledgement before God that the execution of judgment and justice is not your responsibility. It is His alone.

Earlier in Matthew's Gospel Jesus has said, "Woe to the world because of offenses! For offenses must come, but woe to that man by whom the offense comes!" (Matthew 18:7).

In other words, the Lord will deal with the offender in a way that is just. They will not get away with what they have done. Indeed, "it would be better for him if a millstone were hung around his neck, and he were drowned in the depth of the sea!"[13] God will bring judgment to the unrepentant – those who go on in their sin without any concern over how they have hurt others. But we must step out of His way. We do that by refusing to handle the matter in our own way.

A few weeks later, this erring pastor was uncovered in his sins. He suffered great loss.

Belinda and I, and our four children, moved to Boulder, Colorado in June of 1981. We needed healing and restoration from the bitter failure we had experienced during the previous six years. The Lord provided us with loving care through a group of believers known simply as Bethel Fellowship, a small church with a wonderful family atmosphere.

The pastor was fatherly and wise and the body of believers was supportive and very loving. Beyond this the church did not have much structure or any similarity to the traditional model of church government. During the following year the Lord restored us to faith, joy, vision, love and wholeness through the worship, fellowship and ministry of the church.

In June of 1982, a most marvelous thing happened: the pastor of the church resigned to move to a church in Texas. Before making this known to the congregation he shared it with me. He asked me to pray about what the Lord would have me do concerning Bethel Fellowship. I did as he asked and the Lord assured me that it was His will for me to become the pastor of this church.

Accepting the appointment from God, I couldn't help but wonder if the next six years would end in the same kind of loss and disappointment that we had experienced at the previous church. I earnestly asked the Lord about this and He comforted me with these promising words, "There (referring to the former pastorate) you saw what kills a church; here, I will show you what brings one to life!"

With that word resonating in our hearts Belinda and I once again entered into full-time ministry with confidence in the Lord and His promise!

We worked by faith and watched in wonder as the Lord began to move again by His Spirit – touching lives, saving souls, redeeming marriages, strengthening families, building community, and healing men and women from the ravages of sin. We had once again become a part of the timeless work of helping others escape from the biggest prison in the world.

Chapter Seven

The Biggest Prison in the World

There is a Prison without Walls. It has no iron bars, no electric fences, no armed guards, and no gun towers. There are no Nazi searchlights panning the yard at night, for there is no yard. There are no barracks, no grounds, and no imposing gate of any kind.

Nevertheless, it is the biggest prison in the world. It is the Prison of Separation - that mysterious dark power that keeps us apart from one another, and from the God who speaks. The reach of its incarcerating power spans all cultures, includes all ages, and stretches through the very corridors of Time itself, holding entire generations in perpetual captivity.

One example of this occurred around 600BC, during the days of Jeremiah the prophet, who in the words of J. Sidlow Baxter was "one of the bravest, tenderest, and most pathetic figures in history."[14]

Chosen as a young man and fortified with God's word, Jeremiah set forth on the unpleasant mission of preaching a difficult message to a nation of hard-hearted, opinionated, and unrepentant rebels.

He warned them of the coming judgment, but they didn't want to hear it. They tossed him in a dungeon, in an attempt to shut him up. It didn't work. His words still resonated in the hearts of all who had heard them, whether they liked it or not.

And God Himself watched over His word to perform it, seeing to it personally that everything Jeremiah had spoken would surely come to pass. And so it did. The nation that had turned its back on God was taken captive into a land of strange and fierce people - *Babylon*. And they would remain there for seventy years. In prison terms that's essentially a life sentence. And, in *their* case it was without parole.

It was not only a long experience, but a mournful one as well.

"We sat down by the rivers of Babylon, and we cried and cried," they tell us. "We took our harps and hung them in the branches of the weeping willows." That is a fitting picture of just how defeated and demoralized they had become. Even when their captors demanded songs from them, the only reply was a lamentation, "Oh, how could we ever sing God's song in this wasteland?" (See Psalm 137:1-4).

Think about the innocent children who were born to these imprisoned parents during the seventy years of Babylonian captivity. Naturally, being born in captivity made them captives too, even though they did nothing to deserve it. They entered slavery by *birth*, as did their children after them. The fathers had indeed welded the bars of their children's prison cells.

And the same is true today. Adam's choice, which drove him from the Garden all those years ago, set the course for all his descendants - including you and me. We were born into the Prison of Separation, which Adam built.

And each of us has added on to it down through the centuries. We laid the stone and welded the bars for those who would come after us - even though they are our sons and daughters. And while it is one vast prison, it has many cell-blocks and holding tanks. Each is designed to keep us apart from God and from one another.

May I ask you a question? It's a question that's been in the back of my mind for some time; a question that that will not go away; a question which only you can answer.

"Which prison are *you* in? What is *your* cell-block called?"

Perhaps the better question would be, "What *name* would you give to that particular thing that keeps you locked up?" There are so many to choose from.

Take for example my intoxicated stepfather, angry Jim. Yes, he drank excessively, so much so that he would be considered an alcoholic. But that wasn't his cellblock. No, he was imprisoned by *anger*. Obviously something must have happened to him back in his childhood - somebody said or did something that locked him up. And it was probably his own dad.

What *name* would you give that particular thing that keeps you locked up?

Drinking was merely Jim's way of dealing with the pain. But, of course, the sad irony is that he caused even greater pain to others. *Hurt* people, as they say, hurt *people*.

Another example comes to mind. I met a *wolfman* one day. His name was Phil. He had deep set, steely blue eyes tucked under thick, bushy eyebrows and a sloping forehead topped with vampire hair - black and shiny, and combed straight back.

He looked like Little Eddy on "The Munsters," all grown up. He had a pointed nose and a wry, sly smile. When he spoke, you got the sense that he thought himself to be clever. He was never more than three minutes without a cigarette dangling coolly from his puckered lips, while his eyes continually scanned the surroundings for the sign of a woman. *Any* woman.

When he spotted one he froze like a predator sizing up its prey, his tongue hanging loosely from his mouth. A string of drool fell in slow motion, puddling on the toe of his left shoe. "Ooooooo-weeee!" he would squeal, "Look at that fine, sweet thing! Um, um, um; my, my, my."

Phil's buddy, a guy named Dale, was but a pup. Nervous laughter over Phil's incessant crudeness betrayed Dale's secret voyeurisms. I got the feeling that Dale hung around for the scraps after the wolfman struck.

I once heard that the gods we serve write their names on our faces. Phil, the wolfman, served the god of lust - and it was written all over his face.

What *god* do others see when they look at *you?* Greed? Sexual perversion? Racism? Insecurity? Deception? Bitterness? Are any of these the name of *your* cellblock within this vast Prison of Separation? And, did your dad help build that prison?

Perhaps just one more short story will suffice in explaining this prison thing. His name was Tom. No matter how much encouragement, support, counsel and exhortation one could give him - Tom simply could never bring himself to *believe.* The irony is that Tom was a minister. It wasn't that he could not believe in Christ; Tom could not believe in *himself.*

Though called to lead, he was a man of torturous indecision. And because he waffled continually over tough choices, he lost his job and ultimately missed out on a great opportunity. His life was riddled with doubt, but his doubts - one and all - were rooted in *fear.*

That was Tom's cellblock. Not just the fear of failure, but also the fear of success. Is it possible that somewhere in his childhood someone nicknamed him "doubting Thomas" and it stuck?

I wonder if in *any* of these stories an aging father might look back upon the sad life of his adult son, and say, *"Dear God, son, I built that prison!"*

No Way to Spend Your Life

In this vast penal complex of Separation, not only do bad people do bad things, but so do *good* people. Fear crouches at every turn. Guilt and shame lurk in every corner - guilt for what we have done to others, and shame for what has been done to us.

And let me tell you - behind these unyielding walls you will find sorrow that cannot be consoled, hatred that will not be appeased, and a certain emptiness that haunts the soul like the howling sounds of a high wind on a cold and *lonely* night.

Loneliness. That is the insidious condition which is most pervasive in this dark and dreadful place. It is perhaps the ultimate score of Separation's dark power against our fallen souls. "It is not good that man be *alone*,"[15] God said in the dawn of man's new life, and you can be sure that from that moment forward Satan - always contrary to God - has sought to do whatever he can to make man a lonely and miserable creature.

> **Solitary confinement is Satan's ultimate aim for each one of us.**

Solitary confinement is Satan's ultimate aim for each one of us.

"O how doth the heart in the midst of crowds feel frightfully alone!" wrote English essayist, Charles Lamb.[16] The great Albert Einstein perhaps said it even better, "It is strange to be so universally known and yet be so lonely."[17]

It is a widely known fact that many of the most popular entertainers struggle with overwhelming depression and insecurity, brought on by profound loneliness. Marilyn Monroe and Elvis Presley, whose lives ended prematurely and tragically, are two riveting examples. The devil wants to separate you, then isolate you, and finally *terminate* you. Loneliness is the first step into this path of destruction.

Surely, there was never anyone as lonely as the guilty Adam. Just moments after he ate the fateful apple we find him hiding from God in the cool of the day. Separation will do that to a man or woman; it will disconnect you from God and leave you in such confusion that you will actually believe He really cannot see you there, hiding behind the bush.

Some years back I had a counseling appointment with a couple in my church. We agreed to meet in their home and I arrived as planned. I rang the doorbell, but there was no answer. I did it again and waited; still no answer. So I knocked on the door; a good, firm rap to insure it would be heard. No reply. Bewildered, I knocked once more - this time *pounding* the door. "Maybe they are in the back and just can't hear me," I thought.

Then I heard someone from inside say, "There's no one here!" Obviously, they had changed their mind about meeting with me, but sure had a strange way of letting me know.

I wonder how many are like that toward the Lord. He stands at the door and knocks, only to hear a pestered voice from inside say, "There's no one here!" That's what it was like when Adam hid behind a bush in the garden, cowering in the loneliness that his guilt had created.

Cain, a man whose name heads the list of history's notorious souls, knew great loneliness when he was driven from the presence of the Lord and marked with an everlasting curse for murdering his brother. Why did he do so foul a thing?

The Bible tells us that Cain became angry when God rejected his offering of grain. His anger intensified when God accepted Abel's offering of a lamb. Cain was trying to relate to God in religious terms, on the merits of his own works – grain which he brought forth from the ground through the sweat of his brow - and God would have none of it. Religion can make a man lonelier than anything else in the world. Lonely and *murderous*.

And what about Judas on that dreadful evening when he betrayed the Lord with a kiss? We are told, "he went out, and it was night." He moved from the light into the darkness, literally and symbolically. He went from fellowship to separation, from friendship to loneliness, and from honor to shame. Judas walked from life to death, and gave up heaven for hell.

Job felt the suffocating power of loneliness as he sat upon his ash heap, deprived of his children, cursed by his wife, chided by his friends, and mocked by the devil. "Let the day perish wherein I was born," he cried out in friendless grief, "and the night in which it was said, 'A man child is conceived!'" (Job 3:3)

The Psalmist lamented, "I am as a sparrow alone on the house top." Then, he cried out, "Lord, turn to me and be gracious; for I am lonely and afflicted."

The Preacher of Ecclesiastes penned his review of the wealthy man who, despite his riches, was pierced with sore travail because he was *alone*. "For whom do I labor," he cried, "and bereave my soul of good? This is vanity!" And again the Preacher warned, "Woe to him who is *alone* when he falls, for he will have no one to pick him up."

Hosea the prophet recorded one of the worst things God could ever say about any man. "Ephraim is joined to his idols," the Lord said; and then added His sobering verdict, "Leave him *alone*."[18] Who could bear the thought of the Lord passing them by, deciding to leave them alone in their captivity?

"Pass me not, O gentle Savior!" the old hymn says, "Hear my humble cry! While on others Thou art calling; do not pass *me* by!"[19] Isn't that your cry, as you languish in the confines of a life you know is less than what God wants for you?

What if I told you there was a way out; would you want to know about it?

Separation first disconnects us from the God who speaks, then from one another, and ultimately from our very selves. We fall far short of the being who God created us to be, and we live out our empty days in this dreadful prison.

But what if I told you there was a way out? Would you want to know about it? Or, are you one of those inmates who has settled in your cell; adapted to your incarceration, and become content to live a confined and limited life? Surely not! You wouldn't be reading this book if you felt that way.

What I'm saying is simply this – prison, as if you didn't already know, is no place for you! And even though we were born into captivity, we do not have to remain there.

A Deliverer has come; a way of escape has been provided for us.

And I'm going to show it to you in the following pages.

"Lord, You have made us for Yourself," Augustine wrote, "and our hearts are restless until they find their rest in You."[20]

Your very desire for a life of freedom and purpose is a strong indicator that the Lord is already at work in your life. The fact that He has prevented you from finding rest in anything other than Him means that your cries have been heard. You are about to discover that He is more than ready, willing and able to set you free.

And like Israel of old after the Lord had rescued them from Babylon, you too will join the company of the redeemed and sing in great celebration, "When the Lord turned our captivity, we were like them who dream!" (Psalm 126:1)

So, are you ready for freedom? Alright, then; let's bust out of this place!

Chapter Eight

The Great Escape

W e had no way of knowing exactly how many men would show up, but we knew it was going to be huge. However, what actually happened at the National Mall in Washington, DC on October 4, 1997, far exceeded our highest hopes. A massive crowd of men – yes, men *only* – gathered for STAND IN THE GAP, a sacred assembly sponsored by *Promise Keepers*, and by all counts the number exceeded 1.4 million.

The full day's program was developed to help Christian men of all ethnic backgrounds to humble themselves in the sight of the Lord, and offer repentant prayer on behalf of our Nation. The demonstration of unity was truly unprecedented. Indeed, never before in the history of the world had that many men ever gathered in a single place for anything other than war.

Having been an integral part of Promise Keepers from its inception, my role in these proceedings had been to work with others in developing the actual program for the day. We would select and secure the various speakers who would either lead in prayer or bring a message of encouragement to the men. Almost everything was set in place a good three months ahead of time. Only one detail had to be confirmed.

We knew that millions of people around the world would be watching the live broadcast, as well as listening on radio. We wanted to give them an opportunity to hear the Gospel. We prayed that many would trust Christ as their Lord and Savior. Our choice for this part of the program was clearly obvious – who better than the world-renowned evangelist, Billy Graham? We invited him and then awaited his reply.

Meanwhile, I was invited to preach in England at a large annual gathering in Somerset called New Wine. Belinda and I were there for about two weeks before returning home. While we were in England, *Promise Keepers* had heard back from the Graham organization. Because of a scheduling conflict Billy would not be able to participate in our event.

So Dale Schlafer, Chairman of the Board of Directors for PK, extended the invitation to someone else. I was overwhelmed when I learned the name of the new invited speaker; for the letter was sent to *me!*

My hands trembled as I read the letter and my soul shuddered with a dreadful sense of great responsibility. It was a very sobering moment. I knew that there would be people for whom this would be the only time in their entire lives for them to hear the Gospel.

"Who am I, Lord?" was all I could think to ask. Sitting alone in my study with tears streaming down my cheeks, the Lord calmed my heart and filled me with a resolve to make this singular message the clearest it could possibly be. I spent the following weeks leading up to the event doing exactly that.

What you are now about to read is the actual text of that message, just as it was presented on that unforgettable day. I pray that even as you read it, the presence of the Lord will move upon your heart and make it as real to you as it is to me. Imagine you are sitting in a vast throng of more than a million men, and you hear a nameless preacher speak these following words...

There were two notorious and wicked brothers who terrorized a small town in the Midwest. When one of the brothers died it became the other's responsibility to make funeral arrangements. However, he could find no pastor in the county who would agree to officiate at the funeral. It wasn't because they lacked compassion; it was because of the unusual request made by the surviving brother. He wanted the pastor to say of the deceased, "He was a saint." Of course, no pastor would agree to do such a dishonest thing.

In desperation, the brother offered $1,000 to any pastor who would say the words during the funeral, and one minister agreed to do so. He was a prominent pastor of a prestigious church, and the entire community was shocked when they heard of his decision. They all came to the funeral, not because they cared for the dead guy, but they wanted to see if the pastor would really compromise himself for a mere thousand dollars.

How do you measure up compared to Jesus?

When the moment arrived, the pastor delivered the epithet without a stutter, "We all know that Charlie here was a wicked man. He was twisted, foul, perverse and full of the devil. But compared to his brother – *he was a saint!*"

Maybe you are a saint compared to your brother, or to your neighbor, or to someone else. But how do you measure up compared to Jesus Christ? Not so good; for Jesus is God's perfect Man, and we are all imperfect.

Sure, we may highly esteem ourselves in things pertaining to the greatness of man, but the sad and sobering fact is "we have all sinned and fallen short of the glory of God."[21] We are not what God created us to be. Nor can we by our own strength become what God wants us to be. Yet while we are helpless, we are not *hopeless*!

The Bible says that God "commands all men everywhere to repent, because He has appointed a day on which He will judge the world in righteousness by the Man whom He has ordained. He has given assurance of this to all by raising Him from the dead."[22] The God who commands us to repent does not leave us incapable of response. He is rich in mercy, abundant in grace and great in His love.

Indeed, "God so loved the world He gave His only Son that whoever believes in Him should not perish, but have everlasting life."[23]

This famous text, known and loved around the world, makes it unmistakably clear that Jesus is God's only Son. Therefore, Jesus is man's only Savior! As one preacher said, "Christ is not one of many ways to God, nor is he the best of several ways. He is the only way." Jesus Himself said, "I am the way, the truth, and the life; no man comes to the Father but by Me."[24]

Christ is the way unchanging; He is the truth infallible; He is the life everlasting. Jesus is the way that you might be saved. He is the truth that you might be sure. He is the life that you might be satisfied.

We are told in Scripture that "Jesus humbled Himself and became obedient unto death on the cross. For this reason God highly exalted Him, and gave Him the name which is above every name; that at the name of Jesus every knee should bow and every tongue confess that Jesus Christ is Lord."[25]

The Bible says, "There is salvation in no other, for there is none other name under heaven given among men whereby we must be saved."[26] There is only one name that opens heaven's doors and God's heart – the name of Jesus. There is only one name that breaks the power of sin and sets the captive free – the name of Jesus. There is only one name worthy of all praise, and deserving of your allegiance – the name of Jesus.

Far from being narrow and unfair – this is the most generous and fairest of all possible solutions. God did not leave us to ourselves to find a way back to Him – for who among us knows where God is that we could first find Him for ourselves and then chart the path for all others to follow?

God alone knows where He is. God alone knows where we are. And God alone knows what it takes for us to return to Him. The Bible says that God "longs for all to be saved and to understand this truth: That God is on one side and all the people on the other side, and Christ Jesus, himself man, is between them to bring them together, by giving his life for all mankind."[27]

Maybe you are here more out of curiosity than conviction. Perhaps you have come not to pray, but to protest. Maybe you have never had anyone explain to you the Gospel of Jesus Christ in terms you could understand. It is my happy task to try and do just that.

Here is How it Works

The Bible says, "As by one man's disobedience many were made sinners, so by the obedience of one shall many be made righteous."[28] This means that you and I did not become sinners because of anything we did; therefore, we cannot be made righteous by anything we do. Someone else did something and that made you a sinner. In the same way, someone else must do something in order for you to be made right with God.

You see, the Bible sums up all mankind in the lives of two men – Adam and Christ. "For as in Adam all die, even so in Christ shall all be made alive."[29] Adam sinned and as a result all of us are sinners. But Adam does not bear the guilt alone, for we have all turned aside unto our own way. We each are twice guilty. Once because Adam sinned; twice, because we ourselves have sinned.

And this matter of sin goes far deeper than our behavior – it goes to the very core of our being. I am not a sinner because I have sinned; I sin because I am a sinner. Sin is not about what we do; it's about who we are. The solution therefore cannot be superficial and religious; it must be substantial and real.

Have I got good news for you!

The Gospel teaches that God is not interested in merely changing my behavior, but that He is fully dedicated to changing *me*! The Bible says, "If any man is in Christ he is a new creation. Old things have passed away; behold – all things have become new!"[30] You can be born again and made new today through faith in Jesus Christ.

Furthermore, "God demonstrates his love toward us, in that, while we were yet sinners, Christ died for us."[31] And "He that spared not his own Son, but delivered him up for us all, how shall he not with him also freely give us all things?"[32]

Whatever you need to live a godly life you will find in Jesus Christ alone. One man got us all into this mess and so God decided that one man would get us all out of it. God looked down the corridor of time and carefully examined each of Adam's descendants - He looked at you and at me - to see if there was one among us who could stand in the gap and pay the price for our sins. But there was none - no, not even one.[33]

So, God did it Himself! He became a man - the man Christ Jesus. He lived among us; was tempted in all points as we, yet without sin.[34] When Christ died on the cross, it was not to pay the penalty for His own sins, for He had none. Therefore, God took the death of His holy Son and counted it as the payment for all our sins!

Millions of people around the world and throughout history have embraced this Christ with adoring praise, and rightfully so. Is it any wonder that we ask you to do so with us today?

Jesus Christ! He is peerless in His exaltation, unrivaled in His Lordship, incomparable in His grace, invincible in His power, unassisted in His work as Redeemer, matchless in His mercy, adored in His glory and worshipped in the beauty of His holiness. In His birth is our significance. In His life is our example. In His death is our forgiveness. In His resurrection is our hope. In His Second Coming is our consummate glory!

It is true that "the wages of sin is death, but the free gift of God is eternal life through Jesus Christ our Lord."[35] And where sin did abound, grace does much more abound![36] Sin abounds in Adam; Grace abounds in Jesus Christ!

You were born the first time into the consequences of Adam's Fall - you had no choice in that matter. But now, you can be born again and enter into the full benefits of Christ's obedience. Here you do have a choice - and no one else can make it for you. You alone must decide.

Centuries ago a great leader named Joshua stood before a vast assembly in his Nation's Capitol and said, "Choose you this day whom you will serve...as for me and my house, we will serve the Lord!"[37] Joshua's challenge brought revival to a Nation, and his choice to follow Christ brought salvation to his house. Won't you trust Christ today? You can make the difference in your home by following Christ, and together we can make a difference in our Nation.

Saved or Lost

Let me leave you with this as I close. The RMS Titanic, the ill-fated luxury liner, had a passenger list of some of the world's richest and most influential people. She was supposedly unsinkable, yet went down in the icy waters of the North Atlantic on her maiden voyage in the early morning of April 15, 1912. Over 1500 perished at sea; there were fewer than half as many survivors. At shore the names were posted in two simple and unmistakable columns – SAVED and LOST.

This planet Earth, a Great Titan on its maiden voyage among the stars of God's heaven, is itself on a collision course with a great and dreadful Day of Judgment. Though many scoff at the thought, the unthinkable will happen - the unsinkable will sink.

And on that final Day when the names are posted on the shores of glory, we will not be listed according to our wealth, status, fame, achievements, religious affiliation or ethnicity. No. There will be but two columns of names recorded in august and sobering finality - SAVED and LOST. On which list, my friend, will your name appear?

The choice is now yours alone.

The Bible says, "God is not willing that any should perish, but that all should come to repentance."[38] In another place it says, "God desires for all men to be saved and come to a knowledge of the truth."[39] There is no question about God's choice for you – He has already done all that is needed for you to be saved. The choice is now yours alone. The Bible says, "Whoever calls upon the name of the Lord will be saved."[40] That includes you. Won't you call upon the name of Jesus today? Perhaps you are wondering how to go about it?

The Bible puts it in the clearest and simplest of terms – "That if you will confess with your mouth the Lord Jesus, and believe in your heart that God has raised him from the dead, you shall be saved."[41]

This calls for a public confession of a private faith. That's what I ask you to do right now. I've spent the past 10 minutes doing my best to show you how much you matter to God. Would you now take the next few moments to show God how much He matters to you?

If you want Jesus Christ to be your Savior and Lord today, to forgive you of your sin, to reconcile you to God, and to save you by placing His Holy Spirit within your heart and life, empowering you to live a life that truly pleases God and blesses others - then stand, and in the universal sign of surrender lift your hands to heaven and pray with me:

Dear God, I am a sinner. I am sorry for all I've done against you and others. I yield to Jesus Christ as my Lord and Savior. Please forgive me, and change me. Make me a child of God. Fill me with your Holy Spirit that I might live the way You want me to. Thank you for your mercy and your grace. I will live my life to honor you. Amen.

May I be the first to welcome you into the family of God! Now that you have taken your first step into a truly extraordinary life, let me show you how you can so live in this world as to bring great honor to your Heavenly Father.

Chapter Nine

Whose Son is *He*?

The Philistine champion stood defiantly before the army of Israel in the open field, bellowing out his unanswered challenge, *"Is there not a man among you who will come and fight me?"*

There was no answer. The otherwise valiant soldiers of Israel were no match for the towering giant, Goliath. Even King Saul, a man who stood head and shoulders above all Israel, was only a sprout compared to this pagan behemoth. Intimidated by his size, and shamed by his jeers, the men of Israel were not merely unwilling to respond – they were incapable. In fact, the Bible tells us they were terrified.

But then, forty days into the face-off, a boy arrived with a delivery of supplies. He was a shepherd boy, who had been tending his father's flock in the pasturelands of Judah. His father, Jesse, had sent him with a load of goods for his older brothers, who were serving in Saul's army. His name was David. He arrived at just the time of day when, once again, Goliath belted out his defiant taunt - *"Is there not a man among you who will come and fight me?"*

When young David heard this, his heart stirred with a passion for God's honor. "I will fight this Philistine," he said. His remarks were immediately reported to King Saul who then summoned for the boy. "What is this I hear?" Saul asked, "That you will fight this giant? You are but a boy, and he a man of war."

"Once when tending my father's sheep," David answered, "a bear came to steal away a lamb and I slew the bear. Then on another occasion a lion came against the flock and I slew the lion as well. This uncircumcised Philistine is but a dog in comparison; he will not be a problem for me."

Saul consented and agreed to let David go out to meet the giant. But first he offered David his own armor. There is more to this than meets the eye. King Saul, as I already stated, was renowned for his stature; he was "head and shoulders above all Israel." In other words, he himself was a *giant* among his own people. Word must have reached the Philistines that Israel had a giant too. So, Goliath was mustered by his commanders to go and challenge Israel's hero. You know, may the best giant win.

When Goliath stood in the valley taunting Israel, he was actually calling Saul out, "Is there not a *man* among you who will come and fight me?" But Saul was no man; filled with insecurity, riddled with self-doubt, always playing to public opinion – he was no match for mighty Goliath.

But there stood a boy full of faith who would go and fight the giant.

"Wear my armor," Saul said to him. Why do you suppose Saul said this? Is it possible that Saul wanted everyone to think that he was actually the one fighting Goliath, after all?

But Saul's armor did not fit David, and thus the plan fell to the side. The useless armor lay empty on the ground, even as Saul sat empty on the throne. And David, filled with God's Spirit, went into the valley of the giant and turned it into a mountain top experience.

The story of David and Goliath is legendary. There's no need for me to belabor it here. There is, however, one part of the story that is seldom ever mentioned; and in my opinion it is the key to the whole event.

The moment David stood in triumph over the corpse of the beheaded Goliath, with the Philistine army running off in seven directions and all Israel shouting to the heavens, a most curious thing occurred. King Saul turned to Abner, his chief aide, and asked a very interesting question about David.

"Whose son is he?"[42]

> **"I want to meet the father that produces *that* kind of son!"**

One would have thought that Saul might ask, "Who is that boy?" But that wasn't his question. No, he didn't want to know about David, as it were, but wanted to know about David's *father*. His question, in so many words, was another way of saying, "I want to meet the father that produces that kind of a son!" Obviously, Saul had never met such a father as this; certainly not in his own home as a boy.

History does not tell us much about Saul's family life. His dad raised wild donkeys and his uncle was somewhat of an overbearing busybody. We don't know if it was a happy home or not, but we do know that Saul, as a grown man, was still an undeveloped child in many ways. While he had indeed been sired, he had not really been *fathered*.

He was an ambiguous man, appearing kind and humble on the one hand, and yet angry and vengeful on the other. One time he was so anointed by the Spirit of God that he actually prophesied. Yet he also sought counsel from a witch when he could no longer hear God's voice.

Saul was also terribly insecure. In fact, he needed constant affirmation to prop up his temperamental soul. He was impetuous, self-willed, and pretentious. He would weep in repentant sorrow for a deed done wrong, then turn around and do it again without remorse.

Self-conscious about his gangly height, he preferred to not even be noticed at times. In fact, he actually hid among the baggage at the very moment when Samuel called him out to become the King of Israel.

We could do well at this point to ask, "Whose son is *he?*"

Solomon tells us in his Proverbs that a wise son makes a glad father; but a foolish son will cause him grief and calamity, and ultimately bring reproach to his name. I can imagine that Kish, Saul's father, found little consolation from his friends as Saul's reign deteriorated into a national embarrassment. And one cannot help but wonder how often Kish regretted not having been a better father to Saul.

You know - *"Dear God, son, I built that prison."*

After David's victory in the valley of the giant, tensions continually mounted in Saul's suspicious heart. On more than one occasion he actually attempted to kill David while in a demonic fit of jealous rage. Of course, the popular song didn't help matters. "Saul has slain his thousands," the people would sing "but David his *ten* thousands!"

Saul's life came to a shameful end on the battlefield against the Philistines. It was not an honorable death. Rather, he fell upon his own sword in his final, selfish act. And the last words he spoke before dying show the emptiness of his mis-spent life, *"I have played the fool."*

Sadly, there is not much in that story to fill a father's heart with pride. But perhaps there was not much in the father to fill his son with a reason to make him proud in the first place. The one must come before the other.

I once heard a comedian say, "When I was in school, a kid came up to me on the playground and said, 'My dad can beat up your dad!' 'Yeah?', I answered back, 'So, how much would something like that cost me?'"

Evidently some dads are regarded less fondly than others!

By contrast to Saul, may I introduce to you Eleazar, the son of Dodo? I don't know if Dodo was a good dad or not. I only know he had a really strange name. There are only two ways to pronounce it, and neither is very flattering. One reminds you of a stupid bird, and the other, well, you know what I mean.

I can only imagine what high school must've been like for young Eleazar. *"Hey, dodo head!"* you can hear Biff the Bully call out during recess, *"gimme your lunch money!"* I'm only speculating, but the point I want to make is nevertheless true – you can indeed amount to something great, even if your dad was a *dodo*! This is what we learn from Eleazar's story. Let's step back in time and see what he has to tell us.

The morning sun broke slowly over the hillside to cast its golden dawn upon a rather large field of ripened barley, ready for harvest. But instead of farmers with plows and sickles, this field was manned with soldiers carrying swords and spears. They were David's elite fighting force. They were there to keep a raiding garrison of Philistines from swooping down and stealing the crop. But something happened for which they were not prepared. On this day it would not be a small detachment of Philistine soldiers; no, it would be an army of them.

Silhouetted on the ridge of the hill, backlit with the morning sun, the Philistine army rose up against David and his few men guarding the field below. David's men scattered and the Philistines assumed they had won the field without lifting a finger. But as the dust settled they noticed two lone men standing back to back in the midst of the field, swords drawn and eyes flashing, ready for war.

The two lone warriors were David and Eleazar, the son of Dodo. And what happened next is one of those amazing stories from the Bible that tend to sound like fairy tales. Those two men, empowered by the Spirit of God, fought valiantly that day against the Philistines and crushed their army. The Bible says Eleazar's "hand was weary, yet cleaved unto the sword." He didn't stop until the job was done, and the Lord brought a great victory through his and David's efforts.

The place where the battle was fought was called *Pas-Dammin*. It is mentioned only two times in the Bible. Once, when David slew Goliath, and then here, more than twenty years later, when Eleazar stood alone with David in the *same* field and the two of them defied and defeated an entire army.

The word means, "the boundary of blood." Today, we might call it "the cutting edge." It quite literally is the place where opposing kingdoms meet in battle; where men of faith slay giants and defeat demonic forces. Sooner or later your presence is required in that place.

I cannot help but wonder if the thing that inspired Eleazar most was the fact that he was standing with David in battle at the very site where David had slain Goliath.

And, in the same way, can we derive even greater inspiration for our own battles - knowing that we stand with the Lord Jesus, who Himself has slain the greatest giant of them all on a hill far away?

Saul fell in foolish pride, bringing shame to all who knew and loved him. Eleazar stood with David at the place where giants are slain and found a place of great honor in history. Now it's *your* turn.

With that thought in mind, may I be so bold as to ask, "Whose son are *you?*"

What father awaits the honor of *your* life's great endeavors? A father's love ultimately is repaid a thousand times over by the honorable life his children live. "Be ye therefore followers of God, as dear children," the Bible says. The Message puts it this way, "Watch what God does, and then you do it, like children who learn proper behavior from their parents" (Ephesians 5:1).

What Father awaits the honor of your life's great endeavors?

Our Father Who Art in Heaven

One of my first overseas preaching trips took Belinda and me to England, and then across the North Sea into Denmark. Our team stayed at a retreat center near the city of Zwolle, along with a few hundred locals who were attending the conference. We stayed there for a full week, but I wasn't scheduled to speak until the final session on Friday evening.

When the time came, I shared my testimony about being in the prison my father built. Many were noticeably moved as the Lord ministered that night.

The next morning as our team gathered at the bus to head for the airport, several people came to send us on our way with warm appreciation for our ministry and presence there. One man walked over to me and firmly took hold of my hand, holding it with both of his. He was an aged man, wrinkled and weathered with the years, his skin looking like soft leather. His eyes were as blue as the Dutch sky, and *tearful*.

"I must ask your forgiveness," he said, looking me square in the eyes.

"Why?" I asked, genuinely perplexed.

"All this week I've watched you walk about the grounds, smiling and laughing without a care in the world. And I judged you in my heart. *Who is this boy*, I thought to myself, *that he should come here to tell us how to live.* I was sure that you had never known a day of sorrow in your life; born to a good family and raised in a loving home. But then last night I heard your story, and realized how very wrong I had been."

At this point my eyes were filled with tears; I wanted to let him know that I held nothing against him – but he wasn't finished.

"Then it struck me," he said, "*God* has been a good Father to you, and that explains why you are so happy. And now, I want Him to be *my* Father, too."

Jesus said, "Let your light so shine before men that they may see your good works, and glorify your Father in heaven" (Matthew 5:16). You and I can live in such a manner as to cause the kings of this world to ask aloud, *"Whose son is he?"* And we can answer without flinching, "Oh, look and see for yourself just how great is the love the Father has lavished upon us, that we should be called children of God!"

Yes, I am the offspring of Bert Eugene Ryle - a convicted robber and a welder of prison bars. But he was not my *father*. How could he have been; he was never *there*. Indeed, I've had several "daddies" over the years - a stepfather, an odd collection of dormitory parents, a prison warden, and then a few pastors who took me under their wings. Some were better than others; some complete boneheads. Through it all, however, I've really had only one *Father* - heavenly in every way.

The Father of Light has supplied us with every good and perfect gift; we are lacking for nothing! As a good and true Father, He gives us counsel, correction, nurture, provision, affirmation, purpose and empowerment. He has sent the spirit of His Son into our heart, whereby we cry out, "Abba! Father!" Another way of saying it is, *Papa*.

That's God's favorite name.

Chapter Ten

God's Favorite Name

Paul the Apostle was in ancient Athens at the height of its glory, beholding the whole city given over to pagan worship and unbridled superstitions. Seeing one altar in particular, he used it as an opportunity to tell the bewildered citizens about the one true God.

"I see an altar to The Unknown God," he said. "I know Him, and will help you get to know Him, too."

There are in fact many, many names by which God may be called, each revealing a certain aspect of His infinite personality. Here are just a few of the more commonly known names.

- He is *The Lord God Almighty*, showing His sovereign power over all things

- *El-Shaddai*, the God who is sufficient for all the needs of His people

- *Elohim*, the Eternal Creator

- *The Great I AM*, the all in all, all the time in every situation – past, present, and future.

As I said, the whole list is quite extensive and each name is worthy of individual reflection. But there is *one* name in particular that just may be God's *favorite* name by which He is known – *The Father of the Fatherless*. Or, if I may sum it up in one word: *Papa*.

"A father of the fatherless, and a judge of the widows, is God in his holy habitation" (Psalm 68:5). The passage goes on to tell us that God "sets the solitary in families." It is not His doing, nor His will, when children are abandoned in any way; and He intervenes with justice each and every time it occurs.

Joseph, Moses, Samuel, Esther, Josiah, Timothy, and *Jesus*; this lists some the Bible's more illustrious individuals. Do you know what all these have in common? They were raised by stepfathers or by no father at all. God raised them up *Himself* and blessed them each in extraordinary ways.

Stepping outside the pages of the Bible and looking into the annals of history we discover essentially the same dynamic at work there. Some of the greatest and most influential people in history have, in fact, been *fatherless*.

Aristotle, Augustus Caesar Octavius, Johann Sebastian Bach, Leo Tolstoy, John Keats and Rudyard Kipling; Nelson Mandela, Anthony Hopkins, John Lennon, Art Linkletter, Willie Nelson, Marilyn Monroe, Houdini, Louie Armstrong, Bill Clinton, Babe Ruth, and Steven Jobs – just to name a few.

My point in telling you this is not to suggest that all these remarkable people lived godly lives, but rather that God nevertheless favored them with undeniable advantages to insure that they would at least have a shot at a good life. That's how much He cares for the fatherless.

And that's how much He cares for *you*.

A Picture of God

The Bible is a book of pictures; it is a family photo album. But since they didn't have cameras back in those days, they used words to describe what they saw. One key to understanding the Bible, then, is to read the words until you *see the picture*.

OK, so here is a picture of God. We are told that God is Love. And we are also told that Love is patient and kind. Since both statements are true, doesn't it stand to reason then that *God* is patient and kind? Of course!

Therefore, in Paul's famous poem found in First Corinthians 13, he is not *defining* this thing called Love; rather, He is *describing* God - who *IS* love.

With that thought in mind I took a look at what Paul wrote, using every available translation of the Bible I could find. But instead of using the word *love*, I replaced it with *God*. What I discovered astounded me, and I think it will do the same to you.

I invite you to read the following lines slowly and reflectively. But first, brace yourself - some of your thoughts and ideas about God are going to be challenged and, hopefully, *changed*.

> "God is always patient. He waits, and waits, and waits; and does not grow anxious or hurried while waiting.

> "God is always gracious and kind. Always. He does not behave indecently, or inappropriately. There is nothing He would ever say or do that would intentionally embarrass or humiliate us. Never.

> "God is never envious, insolent, or rude. He is not sarcastic in His speech, cutting in His wit, nor condemning in His tone.

> "God is not puffed up, nor conceited. He does not cherish inflated ideas of His own importance. He doesn't walk about heaven fanning Himself, singing, 'Hallelu-Me.'

"God does not behave in an unseemly manner in any situation, or towards anybody. He is never vulgar nor haughty.

"God does not pursue His own things; He does not seek, nor demand His own way.

"God is not irritable or touchy. He is not easily annoyed, nor quickly provoked. He is not resentful.

"God hardly notices when He is wronged, and doesn't even take it much into account when it occurs.

"God does not impute evil on anybody. He doesn't even *think* evil; such things do not enter His mind.

"God is never glad with sin, but always glad to side with truth. He is never glad about injustice of any kind, and He sings the loudest whenever the truth wins.

"God quietly covers all things that could otherwise bring shame and dishonor to your life, and He graciously bears you up under everything that tries to put you down.

"God believes the best about you at all times and in all things, and He will never give up on you. Never.

"His hope is unlimited, His love is unfailing, His commitment is unending, and His power is unflagging - no matter what the circumstances of your life may be, you will find Him there at your side...and *on* your side.

"He will always stand His ground defending you, no matter what it cost Him.

Dear friend, God loves you. He not only loves you *in* what you are facing, but He will also love you *through* it. And in the end, you will love Him for it."

You might want to read back over that a few more times until it sinks in, because the reality for most of us is that we don't think of God in these terms. Rather, when we think of Him it usually is accompanied by feelings of guilt, shame, fear, unworthiness, sorrow - or even worse.

Yet, God is our loving Father and He desires for each one of us to live in His blessing and care. He longs for us to know His presence and sense His pleasure; to experience His power and serve His purpose; to receive His provision and to show forth His praise.

But, not all of us do.

On a Hill Far Away

Though He is our Father, not all of us act like His children. That's one thing the orphanage showed me. Instead of living as sons and daughters, many strive in their service for the Lord as if they were *slaves*. And, indeed they are; slaves to *religion*.

As much as I hate to admit it, I went through such a season in my early years as a follower of Jesus. It was during the time right after I had been released from prison. I was determined to be "a good boy" and make sure everybody else behaved, too.

In other words, I became an obnoxious, intruding, brooding self-righteous know-it-all. You know, one of those guys who brightens up a room by *leaving*.

It took about four years for me to finally burn out and become desperate enough to actually cry out to God. In an odd way I had experienced life from two points of view. One was as an orphan runaway and the other as a duty-bound slave. What God wanted was for me to be His *son*. His Father's love finally won my divided heart on a hilltop in Colorado.

I had read a verse of scripture, which stirred my soul with a longing for God. I really wanted Him to move in a new and deeper way in my life. "You, O God, sent a plentiful rain, whereby You confirmed Your inheritance when it was weary" (Psalm 68:9).

This verse speaks of a time when His people were traversing a pathless wilderness, exhausted and in danger of fainting away. It was then and there that God showered upon them the bounty of His blessings. I was going through my own wilderness, and dared to believe such an outpouring could happen for me as well.

"O God," I cried, "Let Your Spirit come like a plentiful rain!"

"O God," I cried, "Let Your Spirit come like a plentiful rain!" For all of my efforts to serve the Lord in my own strength had brought me to the end of myself; I was spent, and weary and very much in need of a breakthrough. And God, the Father of the fatherless, heard my cry.

It happened during a small and subdued prayer meeting in a cabin atop a hill at the Ponderosa Bible Camp near Colorado Springs. There were seven of us, and we sat around speaking "Christian-ese" for a few minutes before we got down to the business of praying. One fellow began with an appropriate opening prayer, which signaled to the rest of us that it was our turn to follow. So, one by one, the remaining guys prayed, and then it was my turn. But I was spent. There was nothing in me left to give – not even in a simple prayer meeting.

Still, the pressure was on. I had to come up with *something* or else they would think I was, well, *unspiritual*. And therein lay my problem. Everything I had done in serving the Lord up to that point was so that others would approve of me, think well of me, accept me, and see how dedicated I was. But I *wasn't*.

I drew a deep breath and slowly let it out in an even deeper sigh, and then began my prayer with one word, *"Father...."*

And that's all I was able to say, for in that moment something happened to me that I can only describe in the words of scripture as "a mighty, rushing wind." I was overcome by a torrential outpouring of a love from on high, such as I had *never* experienced. I was not simply overcome; I was *overwhelmed*.

It reminds me of the story when the prodigal son returned destitute and ashamed, and his father, seeing him yet a far way off, ran to meet him on the road. The father clutched the beaten boy in the greatest embrace of love ever known, kissed his cheeks and leapt for joy.

That's what *Papa* did to me that night.

I burst into tears, not of sorrow, but of joy. Simultaneously I began laughing with such sheer delight that I must have sounded like a schoolboy on a roller coaster that was way too big for him to handle. It was one of the most undeniable and unforgettable encounters with God I have ever had in my life.

I really don't know exactly how long the experience lasted; it seemed like only a few minutes. But once I calmed down and was able to "enter back into earth's orbit" so to speak, I was alone in the room. The prayer meeting had ended, and the other guys had left. I was alone on the hilltop with.... *Papa* - God's favorite name.

It was shortly after this experience that I was prompted to make the phone call that brought me and my dad back together. And the rest, as they say, is history.

My purpose in telling you this is to encourage you to never settle for anything less than everything God has for you. Yes, you can experience forgiveness of sin and enter into a relationship with the Lord that is wonderful and loving, free from the bondage of the past. But that doesn't mean He finished working on you. There is still much to be accomplished.

Never settle for anything less than everything God has for you!

Having been born again, it is now time for you to put away childish things and learn how to walk in the Spirit. In other words, it is time for you to become a man.

Let me show you what that looks like.

Chapter Eleven

When Does One Become a Man?

W hen I was a child, I spoke as a child, I understood as a child, I thought as a child: but when I became a man, I put away childish things" (1 Corinthians 13:11). This is one of those many quotes from the Bible that made it into the broader realm of world literature. Obviously it strikes a chord in the human heart, a chord that resonates in each one of us.

Every man and woman longs for significance. We want to live a good and meaningful life, to find love and fulfillment, and to have children who will do the same. God placed this desire in our hearts; He wanted these things for us before we did!

We also long for acceptance and affirmation from the two most significant people in our lives – mom and dad; but especially from our dads. For some reason *his* words mysteriously carry far greater weight than mom's. But we live in a fallen world filled with broken relationships. Many of us go through life without ever being accepted or affirmed in any meaningful way.

However, we are not forsaken. God Himself steps in to provide us the acceptance and affirmation we need, often in surprising ways. And these experiences can become turning points in our lives; that moment when a mature self-awareness leads to decisive action that unleashes the potential of who we truly are. That is what Paul means in the two phrases, "When I was a child," and "When I became a man." A *turning point* has occurred. This is something God wants for each one of us to experience.

One night while my aging dad was staying with us during an extended visit, I went downstairs to tuck my two boys into bed. As I passed the guest bedroom I heard my dad's voice through the door, which was slightly ajar. He was *praying*. At first I felt I should go on my way, but something impressed me to pause for a moment. I'm so glad I did. Dad passed away just a few months later and this visit was our final time together.

I leaned quietly against the hallway wall by his open door, listening to a 75 year old man on the threshold of eternity talk to God. I did not realize what was about to happen.

Imagine my emotion when I discovered my dad was praying for *me*! As he spoke my name to God I stood silently listening to him say, "Dear God, I pray for James. Where do I begin? How can I ever thank you for what you have done in his life? You have been a better father to him than I could've ever been. As one dad to another, I want to thank You for what You've done for my boy. I'm so proud of the man You have made him become."

Have you ever had one of those moments when God seems to sneak up on you and surprise you with the totally unexpected? That's what happened to me there in the hallway. My knees buckled and I went to the floor under the weight of emotion, but somehow managed to keep it quiet. I didn't want to bother my dad. There, in that very personal moment the Lord spoke to my heart, "And you thought you came down here to tuck *your* boys in!"

Something happened to me in the hallway that night that began a change in my heart. It was a turning point. My dad saw me as a *man*, and it was time I started to do the same. In the words of John Steinbeck, "It is the nature of man to rise to greatness if greatness is expected of him." My dad's prayer triggered something deep inside my soul; it was time for me to become a man.

Ed Cole, author of *Maximized Manhood*, said to a group of men at a *Promise Keepers* gathering, "Maturity doesn't come with age; it begins with the acceptance of responsibility."

Even though I was thirty-five years old, I was still like a child. I don't mean that I was childlike (that would be a *good* thing). No, I was rather quite *childish* – selfish and juvenile in so many ways. I was embarrassingly irresponsible. The Bible says, "When I became a man I put away childish things." Evidently *that* had not yet happened to me.

> **"Maturity doesn't come with age; it begins with the acceptance of responsibility."**

Yes, I was grown up and had children of my own; I was a respected pastor of a successful church – but I was still a *boy*. And in some ways, a *silly* boy. Maybe you can relate to this yourself. I have spoken to scores of men over the years and know that this is a very common experience.

The phrase "when I became a man" could literally be translated "when I came into being a man." Has that happened to you yet? Have you come into being a man, or are you - despite your age - *still* being a child? That question haunts men well into their senior years.

> "When did I become a man? I really want to know. Sometimes I wonder if I am. Can someone tell me so?

"Was it when I smoked a cigarette out behind the school? Was it when I joined the other guys and acted like a fool? Was it when I took a drink of booze and drove around the town? Was it when I made myself look big by putting others down?

"Was it when I scored the final play that gave our team the win? Was it when I finally got the "A" that made my parents grin? Was it when I had a hot date and we did it all the way? Was that when I became a man? Did it happen on that day?

"Was it when I pledged allegiance to the flag and fought a war? Was it when I came back home and wondered what the fight was for? Did it happen in the Chapel when I walked the wedding aisle? It seemed to for the moment - if we're judging by my smile.

"Did it happen when my kids looked up one day and called me "Pop?" Or was it when I got the job, and made it to the top?

"So now I am a man; at least that's what I'm told to say. But if I am, there's just one thing that still gets in my way. If so, I have to ask it, and the question drives me wild - but, if I've become a man, then *why* do I still act like a child?"[43]

Putting Away Childish Things

Every man must come to that place where he makes the choice of maturity. Manhood is not about birthdays; it's about beliefs and behavior. Paul, a father in the Faith, wrote to his young protégé Timothy, "Let no one despise your youth, but be an example to the believers in word, in conduct, in love, in spirit, in faith, in purity" (1 Timothy 4:12).

These inspiring words chart the course for putting away childish things and coming into being a *mature* man. Let's take a closer look at what Paul said.

First, Paul told Timothy to take personal responsibility for how others perceive him as a man. "Let no one despise your youth," he said, "but be an example." The word *despise* means to dismiss as being insignificant, and Paul charged Timothy to behave in such a mature and manly way that no one would ever have any reason to count him out.

He then specifically identified six distinguishing characteristics of the life that is truly significant; so significant, in fact, that others seek to emulate it in themselves. "Be an example to the believers in word, in conduct, in love, in spirit, in faith, and in purity."

That is the best counsel any father could ever give a child; especially if these six characteristics are already evident in the dad. The word *example* is interesting because it means the exemplar that becomes a pattern by which others are made. Here, then, are six marks of an *exemplary* life.

Your Speech will be Distinguished

The first defining mark of a man who is putting away childish things will be his *speech* - not only *how* he talks to others and *what* he actually says, but his words will carry *substance.* His speech will always be thoughtful and winsome, wholesome and pleasant, gracious and interesting; speech that is above reproach, and which cannot be condemned.

The Amplified Bible says, "Let no foul or polluting language, nor evil word nor unwholesome or worthless talk *ever* come out of your mouth" (Eph.4:29). Somewhere along the way I read that profanity is the futile effort of a feeble mind attempting to express itself forcefully. And someone else said, "Better to keep your mouth shut and have everybody think you're a fool, than to open it and remove all doubt."

The apostle James taught us that if you can tame the tongue, you can control the whole body - just like a small rudder determines where a mighty ship may go. On the other hand, let your tongue loose and you will bring great destruction - just as a single match can burn down an entire forest.

Solomon said, "Careless talk may ruin everything" (Proverbs 13:3, The Message). You know, loose lips sink ships.

A man's words carry enormous power - for good or for evil. With a word you can heal or destroy. You can cut someone to the core of their soul with criticism, or you can release them to heights unknown with your praise.

Do you want to be a man of real significance? Here's your first practical step. Ask God to set a guard at the doorway of your mouth so that no harmful words pass through; only *helpful* words – the kind that builds people up and benefits them in some definite way.

Your Conduct will be Honorable

The second distinguishing mark of a man who is putting away childish things will be his *conduct*; how he carries himself in his home, on the job, in society, in recreation, and in reverence. His deportment toward friend and stranger alike will always be honorable. Such a man is considered a class act, and his behavior brings honor not only to himself, but to all who associate closely with him.

"A noble man makes noble plans," Isaiah wrote, "and by noble deeds he stands" (Isaiah 38:2). The noble man is a *man's* man; and that's the kind of man God wants you to be. Isn't *that* the man you want to become?

Your Love will be Sacrificial

The third distinguishing mark of a man who is putting away childish things is his *love* - how he treats others. The difference between a boy and a man, a child and an adult, can be summed up as the difference between being *selfish* and *selfless*. "Greater love hath no man than this," Jesus said, "that he lay down his life for his friends."

"Yeah, right," you may be thinking, "a *selfless* man? Get real; there's no such thing in today's world!"

I can see why you might reach that conclusion, because there is a great shortage in the earth of this caliber of man. But *you* can be one; you can be different from what has become the norm. You can be released from the prison and walk at liberty as a man among boys; you can walk in love and start a revolution right where you live. Wouldn't that be a good thing?

Your Enthusiasm will be Inspiring

The fourth distinguishing mark of a man, who is putting away childish things, will be his *spirit* - how he governs his passions, and tempers his disposition. He will be a man of inspiring enthusiasm; a man whose spirit is being filled and shaped by God.

Jesus was such a man. The Bible tells us that He grew in wisdom and stature, and favor with God and man. This means He was well-developed mentally, physically, spiritually and socially. God desires that we be the same.

Resolve that you will continue to grow mentally as you age physically, for a man who stops *learning* will stop *living*. Keep your mind sharp and your days will be long and filled with endless discovery. But also take care of yourself physically, for this will add to the quality of life you enjoy. And keep an open door to new friends, as well as old ones; be a man of social grace. But don't stop here.

Paul prayed that we would "be strengthened with might by God's spirit in our inner-man" (Ephesians 3:16). A man who dismisses the importance of spiritual development will never be a complete man. In fact, all other areas of growth are significantly stunted if we disregard the health of our spirit.

I once heard Coach Bill McCartney tell his football team why pre-game chapel was on the schedule. "The spirit is to the physical," he said, "as four is to one."

> **A man who dismisses the importance of spiritual development will never be a complete man.**

In other words, the benefit of developing your spiritual strength is four times greater than merely building up your body's muscle mass. Workouts in the gymnasium are useful, but a spiritually disciplined life in God is far more so, making you fit both for today - and *forever*. (see 1 Timothy 4:8).

Your Faith will be Daring

The fifth distinguishing mark of a man who is putting away childish things will be his *faith* - his ability to maintain unshakable confidence in God at all times and in all trials. Such a man will stand when others falter; he will serve when others quit; he will give when others heartlessly turn away.

A man of faith will be positive when others are negative, up when others are down, true when others are false, and right when others are wrong. Faith is one of the three Olympic virtues, for it "is the victory that overcomes the world!"(I John 4:5). What are the other two? Hope and Love. And the greatest is Love.

Your Integrity will be Commendable

The sixth distinguishing mark of a man who is putting away childish things will be his *purity* - the moral courage with which he lives day by day in the midst of a corrupt and perverted generation. He will be a man marked by purity of character and conduct; a man of private piety and public virtue; a good man, a true man, and a *noble* man. He will be, in a singular phrase, a *godly* man.

Peter wrote, "Abstain from fleshly lust which wage war against the soul" (1 Peter 2:11). And Paul told Timothy, "Flee youthful lusts." If you would be that kind of man then avoid at all cost *anything* that would become scandalous, bringing disgrace to you, and dishonor to Christ.

You put away childish things by *intentionally* cultivating maturity in your speech, your conduct, your love, your faith, your spirit, and your moral integrity. This is a father's counsel to his young son; Paul's words to Timothy; and God's word to you.

By the way, Timothy was about thirty-five years old when Paul wrote this letter to him. So don't dismiss this as something only for teenagers; this is for you.

The truth is that you are never too old to set forth upon this high and noble way. And the sooner you get started the better off you – and our world - will be.

Isn't it time we put away childish things? Let's take a look at the remarkable story of one man who did just that. His name was Josiah. And his example may inspire us to do the same.

Chapter Twelve

The Boy King who Became a Legend

E very boy longs to be a man, and every man longs to be a father. But the presence of sin at work in man's fallen nature has made a tangled mess of the natural process by which this occurs. Pride and greed, hatred and fear, guilt and shame - these dark traits have inherently marked each of Adam's descendants from the beginning of time, as fathers have passed on to their sons and daughters many forms of bondage.

But God has something better for us.

"I have come that you might have life," Jesus said, "and that you might have it more abundantly" (John 10:10). He wants each of us to live a life that is above the ordinary, a life that breaks free from the prisons our fathers have built. He wants us to live a life that honors God and enriches others, a life of true significance.

Consider that kind of life in a young man named Josiah.

The year was 641BC. A great moral darkness reigned over the land, brought about by the godless attitudes and decrees of a succession of wicked leaders. Sexual perversion had become pervasive throughout the empire. And, the people worshipped cosmic powers and sought guidance from the stars.

The Temple of God had been grossly defiled and boarded up, preventing any and all acknowledgement of the one True God. Children were sacrificed in pagan rituals and the popular religion was one of black magic and fortune telling. Séances and ghost stories were the norm of public converse; violence and bloodshed were commonplace. Fear ruled in every quarter.

No, this isn't a fairy tale. It is true. And it all happened in the one place most unimaginable - the Holy Land. Indeed, in *Jerusalem* itself. In the very place where God had placed His Name to be honored, there now stood a carved idol of a phallic symbol to the Assyrian goddess Asherah. It was the ultimate insult against the Lord.

A people called by God's name to be a light to the world had become a nation of sinners.

A people called by God's name to be a light to the world had become a nation of sinners. When Manasseh - the king responsible for all this - died in shame, his son Amon ruled in his stead. But he was no different. He lived in the prison his father had built, and behaved in even more foul and disgusting ways. As a result his servants assassinated him right in the palace itself.

But he had a son, a young boy of the tender age of eight, named Josiah. This boy became king in his slain father's place. A new day was about to dawn upon the darkened land.

God's hand was on Josiah; the boy lived the way God wanted. He devoted himself to the path that King David, his great forefather, had mapped out so long ago. He did not turn to the right or to the left.

What is even more remarkable than an eight-year-old boy becoming king is that a man of God foretold all this about three hundred years earlier. Even the boy's name was prophesied.

"O altar, altar! Thus says the LORD: 'Behold, a child, Josiah by name, shall be born to the house of David; and on you he shall sacrifice the priests of the high places who burn incense on you; and men's bones shall be burned on you.'" (1Kings 13:2)

Three centuries later, that boy was on the throne. And the Lord was with him, as a Father to the fatherless. Protected and nurtured by God, Josiah thrived during the early years of his reign.

One can well imagine the extraordinary impact it must've had on this passionate young man when he heard the ancient prophecy that had foretold not only his birth, but also his very name! By the time he was sixteen he set his heart fully upon the Lord and devoted himself to complete faithfulness. Four years later he set out to cleanse the city of the idols and shrines which his fathers had built.

He wrecked the altars of Baal and scattered the debris and ashes over the graves of those who had worshipped there. He even dug up the bones of the priests who had led the idol worship and burned them on the very altars they had used when they were alive.

Then, after destroying those remaining altars, he ordered the entire Temple grounds and city to be scrubbed clean. The one gravesite, however, which he ordered preserved, was that of the man of God who had prophesied his birth and name.

"That memorial stone there, whose is it?" Josiah asked his aides.

"That's the grave of the Holy Man who spoke the message against the altar at Bethel that you have just fulfilled."

Then Josiah said, "Don't trouble his bones." So they left his bones undisturbed, along with the bones of the prophet from Samaria, who had asked to be buried next to this man's grave.

Emboldened by God's favor, Josiah unleashed a cleansing campaign that spread outward from Jerusalem to several other cities, going as far north as the province of Naphtali. This king was for real and none dared oppose him, for God was with him. By the time he was twenty-six, the clean up was all but complete.

One day Josiah sent three of his key leaders to begin a complete renovation of the Temple of God. One of these men was named Joahaz, the official Historian. A great and enthusiastic effort was well under way, directed by men who were honest and diligent.

While work was steadily progressing, Hilkiah the High Priest found a copy of the Books of Moses rolled up and tucked away in a chamber that had been sealed off for many years. He took the scroll and sent it to Josiah the king with the report, "The job is complete; everything you ordered is done."

Josiah asked his chief aide to read aloud from the scroll. As he read the words of the sacred Book, suddenly Josiah ripped his robes and let out a cry that sounded like a lion in the wild! Josiah realized just how far off course his fathers had taken the beleaguered nation. His heart was horrified at how perilous things were; God's judgment against them was long over-due. The words of the Book moved him to make things right with God.

He acted immediately, assembling all the elders of Judah and Jerusalem, and then proceeded to The Temple of God. He brought everyone he could - priests and prophets and people ranging from the least to the greatest.

Then he read publicly everything written in the Book of the Covenant that was found in The Temple of God, and solemnly committed himself to follow God with all his heart. The leaders and the people followed his example, and a national revival swept the land in its entirety. It stands to this day as one of the greatest moments in Israel's illustrious history.

The Bible gives its own epitaph of this great leader.

"There was no king to compare with Josiah - neither before nor after - a king who turned in total obedience to God, with a repentant heart, and with all his mind and strength, following the instructions revealed to and written by Moses." (2 Kings 23:25)

Some may believe that the world will never again see a king like Josiah. But maybe the time has come for such a man once again. And maybe, just maybe, *you* are that man.

Three Marks of a Josiah Man

Such thinking is not presumptuous on our part, for the Bible itself tells us pointedly, "Whatever things were written before were written for our learning," and the things that happened to them serve "as examples" for us today. (see Rom.15:4, and 1 Co.10:11).

The word *example* means "something that is representative of all, which thereby serves as a pattern to be imitated." Hold any coin in your hand and you can see what I'm talking about. A pattern was crafted and a die cut in metal, which was then used to stamp out the coin in your hand. And the coin you now hold is exactly like the *example*.

That same process works with men just as it works with coins. The Bible is like a mold into which God pours our lives so that in every way we become formed after the pattern of truth. Or, it is like a die pressing upon us and shaping us after its image.

Ultimately we know that God's purpose is that we be conformed to the likeness of His Son. He uses His word to effect that transformation. Therefore - since becoming like Jesus is the ultimate goal - who's to say that being like Josiah on our way there is too much to ask?

Three things strike me about Josiah's defining moment, and these three hold meaning for you and me today. He read the Word, ripped his robes, and roared like a lion. It's now our turn to do the same.

Read the Word

First, if you would be released from the prison your father built then you must read God's Word and find out what *He* says to you. Many voices in our world today prescribe how life should be lived. Some are tantalizing and some absurd. And while the volume ramps up to fever pitch at times, there is always one voice that rises above it all; a voice heard only by the discerning ear. It is the voice of Wisdom.

> "Lady Wisdom goes out in the street and shouts. At the town center she makes her speech. In the middle of the traffic she takes her stand. At the busiest corner she calls out: 'Simpletons! How long will you wallow in ignorance? Cynics! How long will you feed your cynicism? Idiots! How long will you refuse to learn? About face! I can revise your life. Look, I'm ready to pour out my spirit on you; I'm ready to tell you all I know.'" (Proverbs 1:20-23, The Message)

You would think such an offer would be quickly seized, but not so. Instead, there is broad rejection of Wisdom with little regard to the consequence.

"I've called," Wisdom says, "but you've turned a deaf ear; I've reached out to you, but you've ignored me. Since you laugh at my counsel and make a joke of my advice, how can I take you seriously? I'll turn the tables and joke about your troubles!

"What if the roof falls in, and your whole life goes to pieces? What if catastrophe strikes and there's nothing to show for your life but rubble and ashes? You'll need me then. You'll call for me, but don't expect an answer. No matter how hard you look, you won't find me.

"Because you hated Knowledge and had nothing to do with the Fear-of-GOD; because you wouldn't take my advice and brushed aside all my offers to train you, well, you've made your bed - now lie in it; you wanted your own way - now, how do you like it?"

(Proverbs 1:24-31, The Message)

We must not only read the Word; we must *heed* the word. It makes sense doesn't it? If we will not heed what God says when He calls out to us, why should He have to listen to us when we call out to Him?

We must not only *read* the Word; we must *heed* the Word.

I had a friend; at least I *thought* he was a friend. But despite how often I called him, wrote him, emailed him, or tried to get together with him - he would *never* answer. So I stopped. Do you think maybe the Lord does the same?

Rip Your Robes

Second, if you would be released from the prison your father built then you must "rip your robes." What does *this* mean? Let me ask a question. Have you ever sized up somebody by how they were dressed? Or, have you ever dressed a certain way so as to influence the opinions others might have about you? Sure, we all have; we live in an image-conscious world.

Ripping your robes is about doing away with the superficial and becoming real; it's about a deliberate repentance from fashionable living – that tendency of always trying to fit in with the crowd. It's about a strong resolve to live only as the Lord wills, regardless of its lack of popularity. It's about *humbling* yourself in the sight of the Lord.

"Because your heart was tender," the Lord said to Josiah, "and you humbled yourself before Me, tore your clothes and cried before me - I have also heard you" (2 Ch 34:27, Complete Jewish Bible)

Josiah was wearing the royal robes of Israel's monarchy, which by then *symbolized* the moral failure of his ruling predecessors. His act of ripping his robes was not only literal; it was also symbolic. He showed - by his humility, his repentance, and his resolve - that the old was being replaced with the new. *Change* had come to the kingdom.

Let me ask, "How are *you* dressed?" The Psalmist tells us that some are clothed with shame and dishonor, but God wants us clothed with righteousness. Peter writes that we should be "clothed with humility" (1 Peter 5:5).

The prophet Isaiah rejoices in being clothed with "the garments of praise instead of heaviness" (Isa.61:3). In one place Paul tells us to "cast off the works of darkness, and put on the armor of light" (Romans 13:12), and elsewhere he says, "put on the breastplate of faith and love" (1Th 5:8).

The Lord Jesus Himself told us to "be ready for whatever comes, dressed for action and with your lamps lit, like servants who are waiting for their master to come back" (Luke 12:35-36).

A special wardrobe has been custom tailored for each one of us in the kingdom of God. But we must first "rip the robes" that identify us as something other than who God has created us to be.

Because I was raised in an orphanage, for several years I was *clothed* with an orphan spirit. That robe was ripped away on a hilltop in Colorado. I spent time in the Texas State Prison *dressed* as a convict. But I don't wear *those* clothes anymore. Christ has set me free.

Rip your robes! Don't settle for being anything less than the man God wants you to be. Remove anything that would prevent you from fully and faithfully accomplishing His will for your life. Rip your robes!

Roar Like a Lion

Finally, if you would be released from the prison your father built, then you must roar like a lion - unleash the passion in your heart for the honor of God's name, the cleansing of His House, the blessing of His people, and the reviving of a nation.

This goes contrary to conventional thinking. The trend of public debate has all but muzzled the Christian voice, especially the voice of *men*. Because we have often been sequestered into silence, we seem much too willing to quietly go along with the *confinement*.

This is a prison from which we must break free.

Peter and John stood before a tribunal of judges who held the fate of the accused disciples in their hands. The tribunal had ordered them to not speak in the name of Jesus again.

But Peter and John answered the tribunal by saying, "Whether it is right in the sight of God to listen to you more than to God, you judge. For we cannot but speak the things which we have seen and heard" (Acts 4:19,20).

Faced with even greater threats, the emboldened disciples asked God, not for deliverance – but *courage*.

They roared like lions.

After my dad passed away and his affairs were all settled, one prize that I inherited was his old Bible. Several handwritten notes are scattered through its pages; one in particular caught my eye. "Silence isn't always golden," Dad wrote, "sometimes it's just plain yellow."

Dr. Martin Luther King, Jr. said, "History will have to record that the greatest tragedy of this period of social transition was not the vitriolic words and the violent actions of the *bad* people – but the appalling silence and indifference of the *good* people. Our generation will have to repent not only for the words and acts of the children of darkness, but also for the fears and apathy of the children of light." He then added, "Our lives begin to end the day we become silent about things that matter."[44]

> "Our lives begin to end the day we become silent about things that matter."

Amos, the country prophet, said, "The lion has roared! Who will not fear? The Lord God has spoken! Who can but prophesy?" (ch.3:8). One translation says, "even ordinary people become prophets when the Lord God speaks."

One of my favorite old hymns says,

"Once to every man and nation
    comes the moment to decide,
in the strife of truth with falsehood,
    for the good or evil side.
Some great cause, some great decision;
    offering each the bloom or blight.
And that choice goes by forever
    between that darkness and that light.

"Then to side with Truth is noble
    when we share Her wretched crust;
ere Her cause bring fame or fortune,
    or 'tis prosperous to be just.
Then it is the brave man chooses,
    while the coward stands aside
until the multitude makes virtue
    of the Faith they had denied."

(James R Lowell, 1845)

Read the Word, rip your robes, and roar like a lion. A nation's future may hang in the balance. Not to mention your own legacy. Like Josiah, you can be released from the prison your father built and set the course for a new destiny in your family history.

Let me show you how.

Chapter Thirteen

Released From the Prison My Father Built

Dec.December 22, 1970. It was three days before Christmas, and this would be my *last* day in the Texas State Penitentiary. My time spent in darkness was over. The valiant words of Micah the prophet had now become my own - "Rejoice not against me, O mine enemy; when I fall, I shall arise; when I sit in darkness, the Lord shall be a light unto me" (Micah 7:8).

As I walked through the final prison door and stepped into freedom, I had no idea of all that awaited me in God's unfolding will. I only knew that He had carried me through the long ordeal and brought me out unharmed.

Yes, there were days when fears arose and doubts dismayed; nevertheless His word of promise somehow prevailed with sustaining influence in my heart.

"All things work together for good, for those who love God, and are the called according to His purpose." (Romans 8:28).

That single verse had kept me leaning on the everlasting arms through it all. And as I stood there on that public sidewalk in downtown Huntsville, just *outside* the Walls, another single verse was about to launch me forth into the deep.

"Go home to thy friends, and tell them what great things the Lord has done for you, and how He has had compassion on you" (Mark 5:19).

These words were spoken by Jesus to a man we call the Gadarene demoniac; a tortured soul who had lived naked among the tombs, cutting himself with jagged stones, and breaking chains that had been used by others to try and bind him.

What must it have been like for our Gadarene brother? No man ever thinks that he will be the monster in the woods that children are taught to fear - the troll under the bridge, the ogre in the cave, or the creature in the black lagoon. Nevertheless, that's who this man had become, and he was hopelessly ensnared in the clutching hands of a legion of demons.

Then Jesus came his way and, as He had earlier driven the moneychangers out of the Temple with a whip, He dispatched this horde of devils with only a word. Our brother was set free! He was clothed, and in his right mind, and sitting with Jesus! That's when the Lord told him to go home and tell his friends the story.

Obviously, he had friends, for Jesus was sending him back to them. Therefore, he had not always been in this desperate condition; there had been happier days in his past, and there would be even brighter days in his future. The dark season that stretched almost endlessly between the two was at last over, and he was a man with a story to tell.

I can imagine how enthralling his story must've been to all who heard it. "God has not given us the spirit of fear," I can hear him telling the crowds, "but of power, and of love, and of a sound mind."[45] This liberated man was living proof of the Gospel's power; and that is precisely what the Lord wants each one of us to be today.

The old Hymn writer said it best –

"We've a story to tell to the nations,

that shall turn their hearts to the right;
a story of truth and mercy,
a story of peace and light.

For the darkness shall turn to dawning,
and the dawning to noonday bright,
and Christ's great kingdom shall come to earth.
The Kingdom of love and light!"[46]

What is *your* story? It's a question you will need to answer sooner or later. That's the question I first asked my dad all those years ago, and his answer rocked my world. Do you know what your answer is? Have you given any thought to whose life will never be the same once they hear *your* story? Or, has it even occurred to you that you have a story worth telling?

> **What's *your* story? It's a question you will need to answer sooner or later.**

You do; even if you don't fully realize it just yet. God has been present in your life since before you were even born, working all things together for your good. Once you begin to grasp that astounding truth, your perspective on *everything* will change. You will see God's handiwork unfold as He writes your life story. And that, my friend, is something worth telling!

I went home to my friends and began telling my story to anybody who would listen. As it turned out there would be plenty of opportunities for me to do so.

"The Jesus Movement" was spreading across the United States and Europe, with literally hundreds of thousands of young people converting to Christ. It reached its peak by the summer of 1972. This sensational and sweeping move of God gave me a vast community with which I could identify. It also gave a measureless throng of hungry souls to whom my story would bring hope and deliverance.

It never ceases to amaze me, even to this very day, how the Lord works in our lives to accomplish His purpose. Had I not reconnected with my father and heard *his* story, my own story would be incomplete. Neither would I have given much afterthought to the day I was released from prison, other than to say it was a happy day.

Yet, that all changed when the Lord spoke to my heart that night in my father's den.

"I have set you free from a prison your father has built," the Lord said, "and will now use you to set others free from prisons *their* fathers have built. Go home to your friends and tell them what great things the Lord has done."

For the first time, I was able to view my prison experience as something *symbolic*; something that meant so much to me could now have an even greater meaning for others.

Looking back there were three specific things that happened when I was released from the Texas prison. And I believe those things have relevance today for *anybody* who wants to be set free from whatever prison may be holding them.

First, I had to walk through the gauntlet of opposition. Second, I had to pass the test of liberty. And third, I had to step beyond the doorway into freedom. Let's look at each one of these a little more closely.

Walk Through the Gauntlet of Opposition

Even though it is the *one* day each inmate longs for *every* day, when that day actually arrives it is surprisingly unexpected. I'm talking about the day when you are notified that you're getting out of the prison.

Bear in mind that the gap between "management" and "labor" is never so stark as in the prison system! Convicts and prison guards do not form warm friendships; they don't share personal moments, and they *never* put the other before themselves. There are no bulletins posted in the dining hall announcing whose birthday it is, or who is in the infirmary but recovering well, and certainly not who's going home day after tomorrow. Convicts only learn about these things when they actually occur.

The morning dawned as before and the routine cell shuffle was well underway when the unexpected happened for me. A guard's voice boomed out from the entrance of the block, "Ryle!" And then followed up with my prison number, "20-91-32!"

He had my full attention. Waiting breathlessly I then heard, "Down and out!" I realize that in other settings "down and out" is not a good thing, but to a guy in prison these are the sweetest words heard since that day someone said, "Take him away."

"Down and out" is prison jargon for, "pack your stuff; you're going home." My cell door slid open, and it was the only one that did. I stepped into the corridor, holding a pillowcase quickly packed with the few personal items I owned, and began walking toward the guard waiting at the exit.

Then it happened. The cellblock erupted with catcalls, trash talking, name calling, and other unseemly gestures and gyrations that ought not to be mentioned here. There were about a hundred other inmates housed in Cell Block C, with three levels of individual cells overlooking the corridor below. Every guy in there could see me walking toward the door. That was their last chance to take a cheap shot, and they didn't let it pass. As I said, it is not something I can put in print.

But the edited version goes like this, "Where do you think *you're* going? You ain't free and you ain't getting out of here! You *belong* here, and you'll be back!"

But none of that was true, so I kept walking to the door. And *that's* the point. If you will be released from the prison your father built, symbolically speaking, you must stop believing the lies that have been holding you in your cell.

The devil wants you to believe that you deserve to be locked up; that "prison" is where you belong, and that freedom will never truly be yours. *But he is a liar.*

Jesus said that the devil is "the father of lies." Indeed, the first words attributed to Satan in the Bible are, "Yea, hath God said?"(Genesis 3:1).

Satan knew that if he could cause Man to question the truthfulness of God's word, and to doubt the faithfulness of God's character, then the floodgates would open wide to a torrent of his own destructive lies. He was right.

Adam *believed* the lie and unleashed hell on earth, and humanity has labored long under the curse of bondage which that single lie produced. And, oh, how entangled our world has now become by the incessant flood of a billion more lies that followed. That is what Satan wants you to do now: *Believe the lie.*

"You shall know the Truth, and the Truth will set you free!"

On the other hand, Jesus said, "You shall know the truth, and the truth shall set you free."[47] The choice is clear – stop believing the lies, and begin walking in the truth. My dad was seventy-one years old when he made this choice. "Dad, it's not too late to make a right choice," I had said to him – and he *believed* it. That decision changed everything. Dad started walking in freedom that night, and five years later he crossed the river that took him into the Promised Land.

If you will be free, you *must* walk through the gauntlet of opposition no matter how long the barrage of lies lasts.

Even now as you read these words a clattering of voices in the back corners of your mind say things like, "This isn't for you; you'll *never* be free. This Ryle guy doesn't even know what he's talking about. And, besides, even if it *does* work for others, it still will not work for you! Get back in your cell where you belong!"

It's tragic how many actually turn back. Don't you be one of them!

Another Voice, singular in its persuasive power, now stirs your soul with hope. After reading this far in the book your heart has soared at times with the thought that you, too, can actually be free. Indeed you can be. And you *will* be!

Believe *that* Voice, and just keep walking! "Christ has set us free to live a free life," Paul wrote, "So take your stand! Never again let anyone put a harness of slavery on you!" (Galatians 5:1). Take your stand on the truth of God's unchanging word. It's the one and only thing that defeats the devil's lies.

The one sure thing you can do to withstand the onslaught of Satan's lies is to anchor yourself firmly in the pages of the Bible.

"A Bible that is falling apart," said Charles Spurgeon, "usually belongs to a person who is not."

"I have esteemed the words of His mouth more than my necessary food," said Job in the midst of his fiery trial, and God brought him through it.

Life will flourish for the man who delights in the Word of the Lord; who no longer walks in the counsel of the ungodly, nor stands in the way of sinners, nor sits in the seat of mockers (See Psalm 1). Such a man will rest secure, prosper in his work, and become a blessing to all who know and love him. *That's* the man Jesus is calling you to become; and you will get there if you just keep walking.

Pass the Test of Liberty

Once we were out of the cellblock the guard silently led me down the long hallway, a full quarter-mile in length, which stretched along the entire inner structure of the prison. Perhaps no other sight within the prison walls more forcefully exemplified the narrow and restrictive power of incarceration than that long, narrow, silent hall.

By contrast consider the spacious liberty we are given in Christ. "He brought me out into a broad place," the Psalmist sings, "He delivered me because He delighted in me!" (Psalm 18:19). That's *exactly* what getting out of prison is like. But, I'm getting ahead of myself; before we go skipping through the daisies there's still one test we have to pass – it's the test of liberty.

Located near the center of the prison complex was the Administrative hub, where another prison official was waiting for me. Upon my arrival he began asking me a series of odd questions; personal questions which no one but I would know how to answer. Like, "What's your mother's maiden name? How did you get that scar on you side? Where did you live when you were seven years old?"

The purpose of this curious inquisition was to make sure they were clearing the proper inmate for release. For all they knew some other guy may have switched places with me in an attempt to escape. My answers therefore had to be exactly right. If I failed to answer any of these questions correctly, it would have been back to Cell Block C for me.

It is the same way for you now as you prepare for your release from the prison your father built. But instead of a prison guard asking the questions, it will be the Holy Spirit; and He will ask you only one question.

Yes, one question only. Your answer to *this* question matters far more than you may realize, for if you get it wrong you're going back into your cell. And you will stay there until you get it right. Do you want to hear the question?

"Do you forgive your father?"

This is a tough question for most of us to answer, much more difficult for some than others because the pain can run quite deep. Few things scar our lives greater than a father's failures, especially when they tear a family apart and destroy a child's trust. As children we take these things personally, and strangely blame ourselves; carrying false guilt well into our adult years.

The idea of forgiving our fathers does not readily find a place in our bruised and broken hearts.

Once we realize that it was not our fault, the guilt turns into anger – and sometimes, rage. Thus, the idea of forgiving our fathers does not readily find a place in our bruised and broken hearts.

However, Jesus taught us to pray, "Forgive us our trespasses as we forgive those who trespass against us." A good question to ask oneself is "How would I want to be judged if the situation were reversed?"

What if God had given my dad a vision while he had been in prison? Shown him a glimpse into the future, mysteriously projected upon the smoke vapors of his welding flames; and what if he had seen me all those years later - his last son, at the tender age of nineteen - captive behind those very bars he was welding? Do you think it would've impacted him? I surely do.

And what if somehow *your* dad could fully see how much he wounded you with his selfish and sinful choices; don't you think his own heart would break with agonizing remorse? Of course it would.

What I'm getting at is simply this: my dad had no idea what he was *actually* doing. And neither did those who sinned against you. Jesus prayed, "Forgive them Father, for they know not what they do." Can't you bring yourself to pray that same prayer? And besides, how many iron bars have *you* already welded for someone else?

Forgive, in the same way you want to be forgiven.

Every situation in life makes your bitter or better - it all depends upon the attitude you choose to have about it.

Consider the story of Joseph. Hated, beaten, betrayed, and sold as a slave by his very own brothers; he would languish in grossly unjust circumstances until the time came when God made all things right. When God finally exalted Joseph in Egypt, his brothers - who had done great injury to him - stood before him to be judged.

"You meant it for evil," Joseph announced, "But God meant it for good!" His perspective was greater than the wrong that he had suffered; Joseph saw the greater good that God had accomplished through it all. You can, too.

"But you don't know what was done to me!" I hear someone protest.

You're right; I don't. But God does; in fact He knows *everything* about it – especially the things that you do not know, and shall never know until this life is over. So, who better to accurately assess the matter than Him? God alone has the knowledge, the wisdom, and the power to judge your case fully, fairly, and, *mercifully.*

Please understand that extending forgiveness toward those who have harmed you - whether actual or perceived - does not mean that what they said or did wasn't wrong. It doesn't mean that it does not matter anymore. No, rather it is your way of deferring the judgment of it entirely to God and asking Him to be merciful to them.

After all, aren't you hoping in God's great mercy on that day when *your* life is brought before the grand Bench of Heaven? I certainly am! I read in His own Word that "to the merciful He will show Himself merciful."[48] Therefore, I choose to show mercy as much as possible, because I want to receive as much mercy as possible when I myself am judged.

Listen, I'll say it as direct as I can - if you want to be free you *must* forgive those whom you feel caused all the sorrow and loss you have suffered behind these awful bars. Let God take up your case; haven't you been carrying it long enough to see by now the utter futility of your own judgments?

"What is this proverb you have in the land?" God asked Jeremiah, *"The fathers have eaten sour grapes, and the children's teeth are set on edge."* (Ezekiel 18:2)

That saying, which they picked up during their long captivity in Babylon, basically means, "We can't help it if we're this way; look at what our fathers did. It's *their* fault, not ours." The idea behind this pagan proverb is that we can blame *anybody* other than ourselves for the way we live and for the things we are doing. How foolish it would be of me to be bitter against my father for welding the bars to my prison cell. He didn't make it mine – that was *my* doing.

So, who are *you* blaming? Your father? Or maybe, in your case, your mother, your brother, a neighbor, or even a stranger. By holding tightly to a bitter and unforgiving attitude toward those who have hurt you, you only empower them to continue exerting a negative and destructive influence in your life.

Let it go, my friend; for *your* sake, let it go.

Would you take a moment right now and pray something like this –

> *"Lord, I forgive my dad; he had no idea what he was actually doing, being himself a slave to sin – a victim and a victimizer at the same time. Show him mercy, O God, when he comes before You to be judged; the same mercy I hope to receive for all the harm I myself have inflicted upon others.*

> *"Father, forgive me my trespasses in the same measure as I forgive those who have trespassed against me. Let Your mercy make me a better man, lest my own judgments make me a bitter man.*

> *"Turn my eyes away from dwelling upon the wrong that was doing to me, and show me all the good and right things that You have brought about through it all. Amen."*

Heaven applauds you in this moment. A standing ovation! But you still need one more thing before the Hallelujah Chorus breaks forth – you must step beyond the doorway into *freedom*.

Step Beyond the Doorway into Freedom

Getting out of prison is not the same as *staying* out of prison. There is a feeling that comes over a man just moments after the final prison doors slams shut behind him, as he stands unguarded on a public sidewalk for the first time in years. Up to that moment, his every move was predetermined by the strict and inflexible rules of prison life.

My first day in prison set the course for every day thereafter. The bus that took me from Dallas to Huntsville made several stops along the way, collecting felons from various jurisdictions scattered throughout southeast Texas. For that reason a two hour drive took more than seven hours to complete.

We pulled in through the security gates at the Diagnostics Center round about four o'clock in the afternoon. Chained together by ankle irons, we awkwardly left the bus and stood on the pavement inside the prison yard. We were surrounded by about forty unhappy Texas Rangers armed to the teeth, and wearing those infamous silver sunglasses that hid their eyes. You know, like the guy in *Cool Hand Luke*.

A prison guard removed our chains. Then, we were ordered to strip - I mean butt-naked right there in front of God and everybody. Next, this old codger stood on a stool in front of us and made a short speech. He was the warden. His eyes were bloodshot red, and his nose was twice the size of normal from too much alcohol; I had seen this look before when I was a frightened boy on the run from angry Jim. But there was no running away from this guy.

"You men are no longer citizens of the United States of America," he started, in a high pitched nasal drawl famous among Texas ranchers accustomed to talking to cows. "You are now the property of the Texas Department of Correction, and we will do with you as we damn well please."

No one said a word as he continued. "We want to make sure you do not bring anything into our fine institution – weapons, drugs, contraband, or diseases – so we are going to search you thoroughly. This will include a full body cavity search, and if we find anything – it will not be well with your soul."

"We will then shave your head, shower you down and spray you with a chemical solution which will decontaminate you from any germs you may have picked up in your sorry life of crime. This chemical will not harm you," he concluded, providing no comfort whatsoever, "but it will discolor the bricks, so keep your damn hands off the walls!" He wasn't joking.

Then, before marching us into the hose-down zone he gave one final word of warning, "Don't even think about trying to escape; for we will not hesitate to shoot you dead."

Surreal is the only word that describes how I felt that day, standing naked in the middle of the Lone Star State. Then and there I fully understood what they meant when they said, "Don't mess with Texas!" From that moment on it was "yes, boss," or "no boss."

As we fast-forward several months ahead to the date of my release, the contrast between the first day in and the first day out was stark. Standing fully clothed outside the Walls on a public sidewalk in Huntsville, Texas, watching traffic pass by – a profound sense of personal responsibility suddenly hit me head-on with the force of a Mack truck.

I knew in my gut that from that moment on what happened next would be entirely up to me. No boss man would tell me when to work, when to eat, when to come and when to go. And I must confess that, for a brief moment, something in me wanted back inside the Walls. The security inside - yeah, OK, it was *maximum* security - was comfortable compared to the unexpected feeling that real freedom brings.

With freedom comes risk and uncertainties; there are no set deals. In freedom there is no regimen like that inside the confines of marshaled prison life.

And this marks my third analogy: in order to be released from the prison your father built, you must accept the personal responsibility that comes with freedom. In other words, there is no one else to blame but you if it doesn't work out. But, this doesn't mean you are left alone in this daunting quest.

With freedom comes risk and uncertainties; there are no set deals.

Jesus promised, "I will not leave you as orphans; I will come to you" (John 14:18). He also said, "I will ask the Father to give you a Friend who will always be with you; the Holy Spirit!" And it is precisely at this point that the Gospel shines the brightest, for it offers what can be found nowhere else - the power of the Holy Spirit inside you, enabling you to live as God would have you live.

"Walk in the Spirit," the apostle Paul says, "and you will not fulfill the lust of the flesh."[49] The prophet Isaiah gave us this unfailing promise, "When you turn to the right or to the left, you will hear a voice behind you saying, 'This is the way; walk ye in it.'"[50] You can hear God's voice and experience God's power as you walk into freedom.

There is an old adage that says, "The journey of a thousand miles begins with one step." Take that step as you walk through the gauntlet of opposition by believing the truth. Then take another step as you pass by the probing inquisitor, forgiving your father so that you can go forward in life. And then, take yet one more step beyond the doorway of your prison into the freedom Jesus gives you, by receiving the friendship of the Holy Spirit and the power He supplies for you to live a life of personal responsibility.

Summing it up, Solomon gave what may be considered not only the best advice, but the clearest counsel that can be found on this matter.

> *"Trust God from the bottom of your heart," he wrote, "don't try to figure out everything on your own. Listen for God's voice in everything you do, everywhere you go; He's the one who will keep you on track. Don't assume that you know it all. Run to God! Run from evil! Your body will glow with health, your very bones will vibrate with life!"*
>
> (Proverbs 3:5-8, The Message)

Can you *feel* it? You are free, my friend! And now you are ready to begin living your *own* extraordinary life.

Chapter Fourteen

The Extraordinary Life

H ave you ever been in a place where the phone kept ringing and nobody answered it? In moments like that it seems everybody is busy with something else, assuming that somebody else will answer the call. But nobody does. After awhile it can get to be quite annoying. There is something irritating about an incessant, unanswered call.

Over the years I have noticed a similar thing in the lives of many people - a call that is not being answered. A call from the God who speaks. Busy with so many other things, and sure that the call is for someone else, many men lose themselves in trivial moments and miss the momentous opportunity to answer the call of God on their lives. Have you answered the call?

Missing out on God's call for your life would be the worst thing that could happen. Research shows that one of the greatest fears men face is living a meaningless life, a life that didn't matter, a life that made no difference. This dreadful thought haunts even the most accomplished of individuals.

Maybe it haunts you even now.

Indeed, few things could be more unsettling than to get to the end of life, cast a cautious glance back over time and discover what has been suspected all along, *"My life didn't matter!"* Each of us long to know that our lives counted, that we accomplished what we were put on this earth to do. We want to maximize every opportunity, seize the day, and live life to its fullest.

Yet, in an odd contradiction to this universal desire, nothing is more common among us than unrealized potential. Most of us settle for far less than we are capable of being, and of doing. On the one hand we want our lives to count. On the other hand, we seem far too willing to become marginalized into mediocrity. Our only hope is to answer the call of God upon our lives.

Nothing is more common than unrealized potential.

There was this guy out driving in his car when it began to snow. He panicked at the thought that he might become stranded and freeze to death. Remembering the advice of a friend, he stopped his car and waited for a snowplow to come along. Once it did, he pulled in behind the vehicle and started following it to safety. After about forty-five minutes, the snowplow driver stopped and walked back to the guy in the car.

"Mister, are you alright?" he asked him.

"Sure," the guy said, "a buddy told me if I was ever caught in the snow I should follow a snowplow to safety. So that's what I'm doing."

"Well, that's fine with me," the snowplow operator replied. "I'm all done now with the Wal-Mart parking lot; if you want to follow me over to K-Mart, come on!"

Some guys just don't get it! They keep going around and around in circles, supposing they are actually headed somewhere – but they are not.

That reminds me of another guy who wanted to go on a cruise, but couldn't justify spending that much money for a fancy boat ride. Then one day he saw a notice posted at work: "Midnight cruise on Luxury Liner! First Class cabin accommodations, dining with the Captain, all other on board amenities included. $500!! Bring cash in hand to Dock C at midnight ready to set sail!"

He could hardly believe his eyes; this was the deal of a lifetime. So, with cash in hand he showed up as advertised. But there was no boat and nobody in sight. Wondering if he had misread the flyer, he suddenly got conked on the head and knocked flat out. The poor guy woke up the next morning, with a knot in his head, floating in a rowboat in the harbor, and all his money was gone.

Looking around, he saw another guy floating in a rowboat about twenty yards away, with a knot on his head as well.

The first guy called out, "Hey, do they serve breakfast on this cruise?"

The second guy answered, "No, I don't think so. At least they didn't last year!"

Like I said, some guys just don't get it! No matter how many times they get knocked about and left floating aimlessly in Life's harbor, they keep going back for the same thing over and over again.

If you always do what you've always done, you'll always get what you've always got. Thus, if you want something you've never had before, you must be willing to do something you've never done before. In a word, you must be willing to *change*. And change is what happens when you respond to the God who speaks.

Abraham traveled into the unknown, Joseph remained faithful in Egypt, Moses crossed the Red Sea, Joshua conquered the Promised Land, David slew a Giant and became a King, Isaiah told his visions, Zechariah told his dreams, Daniel stood in the Lion's den, Josiah brought revival, Zerubbabel rebuilt the Temple, Nehemiah rebuilt the Walls, Simon Peter left his fishing nets, Paul preached the Gospel and planted churches, and John wrote the Revelation - each one answered the call on their lives.

Each one of those men heard God's voice and followed Him with trusting hearts.

Now it's your turn.

God is in the business of making ordinary people into extraordinary individuals. He does it through the transforming power of Truth. This is what He wants to do with you.

"Follow Me," Jesus said to Simon Peter, "and I will make you a fisher of men." Peter did so and stepped into history. We may do the same today. While you may not regard yourself as an extraordinary individual, you can nevertheless witness many extraordinary things as you seek to faithfully follow Jesus, our extraordinary Savior.

The Bible says "God did extraordinary miracles through Paul" (Acts 19:11). Who is to say He can't do the same through you? And, besides, why not wait until it's all said and done before you sell yourself short? You may very well be much more extraordinary than you think, especially in light of the amazing grace He has given to you.

Years ago in the Dallas County Jail, as I awaited my fate, the entrance of God's word into my desperate heart filled me with light and hope.

"All things work together for good," He said, "to those who love God, and are called according to His purpose" (Rom 8:28).

Suddenly I realized that God had a *purpose* for my life; just as He does for *your* life. The original Greek word translated "purpose" is *prothesis*. And it means "a setting forth in His presence."

This is a veiled reference to the Old Testament practice of placing the showbread on the altar in the Holy Place before the Curtain, absorbing the glory of God before being eaten by the priests. What a rich thought! Our lives are to be like this in today's world; so filled with the presence of the Lord that others experience Him for themselves when they are around us.

The classic poem by A.S. Wilson says it best,

"Not merely in the words you say,
not only in your deeds confessed;
but in the most unconscious way
is Christ expressed.

Is it a beatific smile,
a holy light upon your brow?
Oh no; I felt His presence
when you laughed just now."

The word *prothesis* also means that God's purpose for our lives was completely set in place before we were even born. The Bible tells us that He "chose the exact time and place of our birth" (Acts 17:26). In other words, you arrived just in time at the right place, and in the right family, to get in on God's wondrous plan for *your* life.

You arrived just in time at the right place, and in the right family, to get in on God's wondrous plan for your life.

So what's the problem? Obviously this "wonderful plan" doesn't always seem as clear in every life as it should be. What's preventing it? I suggest that many of us have unwittingly rejected God's *prothesis*, and settled for two other options instead – the first is a *hypothesis*, and the second an *antithesis*. Let me explain.

A *hypothesis* is an unproven theory. It's an idea, maybe even a good one; but it is not real. It's make-believe; it's wishful thinking. It's daydreaming or, in its worst form, it's a vain-imagination. *Hypothesis* is the plan we have for ourselves, independent of the Lord. It's our attempt at besting God, supposing that we can come up with a purpose for our own lives that is greater than His.

Yeah, right. But, c'mon, it really doesn't take you long to discover just how wrong you are, does it? Still, we hammer stubbornly onward, becoming smaller and smaller with each willful step in the wrong direction.

And if that isn't bad enough, we are tampered with by an unseen enemy who is hell-bent on our complete ruin. Thus, an *antithesis* enters the storyline of our lives. What this means is that we have *God's* plan for our lives, which now is in conflict with two *other* sets of plans – our own, and the devil's.

Neither of those can compare with the first, yet most of us choose either of them instead of going God's way. And the results are always disastrous in the end.

God wants you to be a blessing; Satan wants you to be cursed and to cause curses everywhere you go. God wants you to have a loving family and many friends. Satan wants you to be completely alone. And he will use your own odious failures to drive all others away from you.

God wants you to know Jesus and to be filled with the Holy Spirit, doing good and making a difference in your world. Satan wants you to be full of yourself, knowing nothing at all, and living a life that ultimately proves to be meaningless. "The smallest package," someone said, "is a man totally wrapped up in himself." Yep, that's what the devil desires for you. *Solitary confinement.*

The best thing you can do for your life, and for the future generations that come from you, is to answer the call God has upon your life. It is a call to a *person*, Jesus Christ; a call to give your life over to Him by faith, trusting Him to make you the person God created you to be.

It is also a call to a *purpose* greater than yourself; a *purpose* for which you are gifted and in which you will be empowered once you say "yes."

"I know the plans I have for you," declares the Lord, "plans to prosper you and not to harm you, plans to give you hope and a future" (Jeremiah 29:11). Sounds like a plan to me! An *extraordinary* plan!

Now, at the risk of seeming overly simple, let me offer five easy questions you can ask yourself. I believe these questions will help you find and fulfill God's purpose for your life. However, you must be completely honest with your answers in order for this to work for you.

Question #1 - *What is my deepest desire?*

What do you really, *really* want to do with your life? What are your deepest and most cherished hopes and dreams? What is it that you deem to be a worthy use of the one life you have been given? Answer freely here, for there are no restrictions on dreams. If you could be anything and do anything with your life - what would that be?

"Delight yourself also in the LORD," the Bible says, "and He shall give you the desires of your heart. Commit your way to the LORD, trust also in Him, and He shall bring it to pass" (Psalm 37:4-5).

When we put God first in our lives, He fills our hearts with an intuitive hunger for that which He has created us to be and to do. He guides our steps and leads us to the place where a door opens to our future and we see what God wants us to become. When we agree with what we see, God sets it in motion and it surely comes to pass. It may take years to fully actualize, but it will be worth every minute along the way!

> **A door opens to our future and we see what God wants us to become.**

My moment came when I was about twenty-one years old. A preacher came to town and I went to hear him. The guy was simply amazing. His sermon was unlike any I had ever heard; he *transported* me with his words. Time seemed to suspend as my imagination walked the shores of Galilee with Jesus. Once the sermon ended, I stood silently at the back of the church, watching several people gather around the young minister, thanking him for such a moving message.

"Lord Jesus," I said, as if He were actually standing there next to me, "*that* is what I want to do with my life."

I wanted to preach in such a manner that others would be transported by the power of truth, so as to give and live their best for Christ. And now, all these years later, that is exactly what He has let me do.

Obviously, that is what He wanted for me long before I even knew it. So, on that unforgettable Sunday morning I saw the door to my future open and stepped into that which God had already purposed for me to be and to do. That's how it happens.

"This is my life work, helping people understand and respond to this Message. It came as a sheer gift to me, a real surprise, God handling all the details. When it came to presenting the Message to people who had no

background in God's way, I was the least qualified of any of the available Christians. God saw to it that I was equipped, but you can be sure that it had nothing to do with my natural abilities. And so here I am, preaching and writing about things that are way over my head, the inexhaustible riches and generosity of Christ"

(Ephesians 3:7-8, The Message)

Thanks Paul; that is *exactly* what I am trying to say!

The Bible says, "For God is working in you, giving you the desire to obey him and the power to do what pleases him." (Philippians 2:13)

Did you catch that? God gives us the desire *and* the power to do His will. If you will say "yes" to His purpose, He will empower you to do it in such a way that satisfies your deepest longings. In the movie, *Chariots of Fire*, Eric Liddell, Olympic champion and Scottish missionary, said, "God made me fast, and when I run I feel His pleasure."

What is it that, when you do it, you feel God's pleasure over your life?

We are never happier than when we are expressing the deepest gifts that are truly us. When you answer God's call you step into a process of unending discovery and delight. Indeed there are difficulties along the way, but God gives you the grace to face it, the wisdom to solve it, the resolve to overcome it, and the joy of having done so.

The first step on this wondrous journey is desire; what do you really, *really* want to do with your life?

Find the answer to *that* question before you take another step. For if you get this one wrong, everything that follows will already be offline - leading you along a path that ends in a prison called *Separation*.

Question #2 - What abilities do I actually possess?

There is a big difference between wanting to do something, and actually being able to do it. So the second honest question you must ask yourself is, "What skills, abilities and talents do I *actually* possess?" Remember the verse we just read, "God is working in you, giving you the desire to obey him and the power to do what pleases him."

Desire is not enough; you must also have the *power* to do it. Otherwise, your dream is not from God.

Before the call to preach entered my heart I had other youthful aspirations, but clearly did not possess the abilities to pull them off. As a thirteen-year-old boy in the orphanage, catching glimpses of the four lads from Liverpool on TV, my young heart was captured. I wanted to be a Beatle!

I combed my hair forward, got a cheap guitar, learned how to play a few chords, and then made the biggest mistake of all – I started singing. Dang. There was no way I would ever be able to be a Beatle, and I knew it. I sounded more like Tiny Tim tip-toeing through the tulips! Obviously God did not give me the skills, the abilities, or the talents to pursue a successful career in pop music; and the world is a much better place as a result.

God made you for something special, and when you find out what it is, then you feel special in doing it.

Dwight D. Eisenhower, the 34th President of the United States, said, "When I was a small boy in Kansas, a friend of mine and I went fishing and as we sat there in the warmth of the summer afternoon on a river bank, we talked about what we wanted to do when we grew up. I told him that I wanted to be a real major league baseball player. My friend said that he'd like to be President of the United States. Neither of us got our wish."[51]

Evidently, Ike could not play baseball as well as he had hoped! But the diminishing of one dream led to the fulfillment of another - one that was far greater!

So, ask yourself, "How has God wired me? What is it that I can really do, and do really well?" By the way, it never hurts to get input from trusted friends on this one, because they may know better than you whether you are really all that good in a particular skill....or not.

Question #3 - *How do others honestly respond?*

When a new restaurant opens, many people go and check it out. Within a few days, or weeks, it will be evident if the restaurant will *remain* open. People respond positively to that which benefits them, and negatively to that which does not.

So, how do people respond to you when you do the thing you dream of doing?

Do others see the worth of what you bring? Does the door of opportunity seem to naturally present itself for you to do what you desire? Or, are you trying to force it open? Are you becoming frustrated because no one will give you a break? Is it *their* fault that you are not successful? (A violin now plays softly in the background as we all pause and offer a collective sigh for how unfair life has been to you).

Now, if you're finished with blaming others and really want to make a difference, dust yourself off and get back on the horse. You've got the goods; so let's see what you've got!

Walt Mason, an American poet of an earlier time, said it best. "There is a man in this world who is never turned down, wherever he chances to stray. He gets the glad hand in the popular town, or out where the farmers make hay. He is greeted with pleasure on hot desert sands, or deep in the aisles of the woods. Wherever he goes, there's a welcoming hand - *he's the man who delivers the goods.*[62]

The Bible says, "A man's gifts will make room for him, and bring him before great men" (Proverbs 18:16). When you've got the goods, as they say, the doors of opportunity will open and people will receive what you have to offer.

Maybe you have the *desire* and the *ability* to do something in particular, but the *opportunity* to do it never comes. Perhaps it could be a question of timing; maybe you're not yet ready. Or, perhaps this is God's way of redirecting your life back to His better choice for you. Let me illustrate this with the story of a young woman I know.

Her eyes sparkled bright with the full enthusiasm of any high school graduate. "I want to go to college," she announced, "to study theater and business."

"But, that's not the path I've chosen for you," the Lord politely replied.

That was a defining moment. Her love for God and her trust in His faithfulness made a difficult choice somewhat easier. "Alright, then," she answered, "I will lay it down for You."

Her youthful heart began to expand with all the inquisitive expectancy that faith and dreams together can muster. "How far can I go? What languages can I learn? Where might God take me in this world?" Believing that God was leading her to step outside the security and comfort of America, she moved to another country when she was twenty-two. And people responded graciously, opening doors of opportunity for her abroad.

Several years have passed, and that girl is now a woman seasoned with grace and experienced in life far beyond what any school anywhere could ever teach. She has lived in England, Austria, and Thailand. She has now lived in Hong Kong for the past twelve years. She has even started her own business making and selling exquisite handbags, purses, jewelry and other accessories.[53] Her name is Annalisa; and her mother and I could not be more thrilled with how God is blessing and using our *daughter*.

You can well imagine how Annalisa's heart must have soared the night she took center stage in a theatrical production called *"Chasing the Dragon."* It is based on the true-life story of how the infamous Walled City of Kowloon was transformed by the power of the Holy Spirit through the tireless efforts of a lady named Jackie Pullinger. Annalisa played the lead role to a packed house in the Hong Kong City Concert Hall.

Belinda and I were there, watching through eyes blurred with tears. The girl, who wanted to study theater and start a business, is now a businesswoman in Hong Kong, using her theatrical abilities to share the story of Jesus with others. *Extraordinary.*

When we let God choose our inheritance for us, His choice is always excellent. The Lord opens doors that no man can close and He closes doors that no man can open. If you set your desire upon doing what God has called you to do, the opportunities will come in abundance. He will provide you with great and worthwhile work.

Question #4 - *What difference does it really make?*

Few things would be more difficult to hear than the words Jesus said to His taunting brothers, when they chided Him for staying away from the Feast in Jerusalem. "It is not yet My time to go," He said, "but you can go; for your presence there will make no difference" (John 7:6, The Living Bible).

One of the most disturbing thoughts possible is that one's life made no difference. That's what would happen if you settled for something less than His best for your life.

Ask yourself these questions:

"What difference could my life make in the hands of Jesus? What desires has He placed in my heart? What abilities has He placed in my hands? What am I doing with them?

Another way to approach this is to ask, what would be lost to the world if I did not do what God has gifted me to do?

Rick Meyers, a friend of mine, has done an extraordinary thing. Several years ago he was employed as a machinist in Oregon, where he worked the night shift on an assembly line in a blue-collar, dead end job.

What would be lost to the world if I did not do what God has gifted me to do?

"Wait a minute," he said to himself one night, "this isn't working for me. I can't do this for the rest of my life."

So, Rick bought a computer and began teaching himself programming. He obviously had a knack for this and doors began to open. A company hired him to help develop software that operated their equipment. That gave him the opportunity to learn the skills necessary to find and fix bugs in the programming modules. His abilities increased, as did his opportunities.

He began traveling the country conducting seminars and workshops; training others how to use the software he had developed. One of those trips brought him to Tennessee, where the doors opened for another job. He and his family sensed this was a move they should make.

Once in Tennessee, settled in his job and a healthy church, he found himself struggling with a popular Bible software program. "Wait a minute," he thought to himself, "why don't I just write my own study program?" And that's what he did.

He sent copies of it to a few pastors and friends, to get their input on how to make it even better and more user-friendly. After a few tweaks, Rick launched his Bible software program online, offering it completely free of charge to anyone who wanted it.

That was in the year 2000. Right now, as of this writing, over 10 million downloads in 170 countries around the world have occurred. Just in one month, the bandwidth use averages fifteen terabytes - that's 15,000 *gigabytes.* That's a whole lot! You can download your own copy online.[54] In my opinion it is indisputably the best Bible study tool available today. And it is *free.*

God has not only blessed the works of his hands, but the Lord has also poured great blessings upon Rick and his family. He found out what God had wired him to do, and he has done it with extraordinary success.

God alone knows the eternal effect that Rick's decision has had in the lives of millions. But, we can be sure of this one thing - much would have been lost to this world had he settled for the night shift in Oregon.

Is that what you're doing? I hope not. I pray with all my heart that God stirs you to action as you read this book. I pray that the desires and abilities He has placed in your life – to honor Him - will ultimately make a lasting difference in our world.

Jesus said, "You know a tree by its fruit" (Matthew 7:16-20). Fruit is another word for results, which is the *produce* of your life and labor. What fruit is your life producing? Good fruit or bitter fruit? When you do God's will in God's way the fruit which your life produces will be sweet and lasting. This brings us to the final question.

Question #5 – Does this truly energize me to go the distance?

Is the thing that you desire to do so deeply satisfying that you need look no other place for something else to do? Are you *energized* by doing this thing with your life? Jesus said, "My meat is to do the will of Him that sent me, and to finish His work." God supplies us with regenerating power when we expend ourselves in the accomplishing of His will.

Paul said, "I have fought a good fight, I have finished my course, I have kept the faith" (2 Timothy 4:7). One translation says it this way, "I have run the *full* distance."

Can you go the *full* distance in this thing you desire to do with your life? Or, will something else along the way divert your affections and aspirations, turning you aside to other pursuits? Jesus said, "I have finished the work You gave Me to do" (John 17:4). He was single-minded in His focus, and unwavering in His obedience.

President Eisenhower said, "We succeed in life as in war, only as we are able to identify a single, over-riding objective; and then bend all other considerations to that one thing."[55] For me, that one thing is helping you experience God's presence. I want you to hear His voice and find the power to do whatever He is calling you to do.

"One thing have I desired of the Lord," King David writes, "and that will I seek after; that I may dwell in the house of the Lord all the days of my life, to behold the beauty of the Lord and to inquire in His Temple" (Psalm 27:4). By setting himself upon this *one* thing, God blessed David with profound influence in many things.

If you want to go the distance, you must be done once and for all with *indecision*. Set your sights unerringly upon that one thing which the Lord has placed in your heart for you to do – and do it wholeheartedly until there is nothing left in you.

When you take the path that God has chosen for your life you will have what it takes to go the distance and finish well.

The Reverend Billy Graham strikes me as the best modern day example of this truth. "My one purpose in life," Billy says, "is to help people find a personal relationship with God, which, I believe, comes through knowing Christ."[56]

Jesus said, "Go ye into all the world and preach the Gospel to every creature." Billy Graham has done just that – he has preached the Gospel to more people in live audiences than anyone else in history - nearly 215 million people in more than 185 countries! Hundreds of millions more have been reached through television, video, film, and webcasts. His ministry has spanned over 60 years. Seven US Presidents, along with several other Heads of States, have sought his counsel. He is regularly listed by the Gallup organization as one of the "Ten Most Admired Men in the World." Truly *extraordinary*.

Nothing is more compelling than the unflagging spirit of a man or woman who is energized by God's purpose. *"I can't believe I get to do this everyday,"* is the frequent comment of those who have answered the call of God upon their lives and are fully engaged in expending themselves to accomplish His will.

My friend, David Schafer, former VP of Sales for Western Digital, is one of those delightful individuals who makes a difference *everywhere* he goes. He is filled with an infectious enthusiasm for life and a genuine affection for everyone he meets.

"Why are you so happy all the time?" people often ask him. And his answer never varies from this, "I know why I'm here and I know where I'm going."

This often takes the conversation to another level as people wonder what he means by that. "I'm here to honor God by sharing the love of Jesus with others," he says, "and I'm going to heaven to be with the Lord."

And trust me when I tell you this – there is no way you will ever meet Dave Schafer without being hugged!

The bottom line is this: Everybody needs a place to serve, and service that matters. Os Guinness said, "Our passion is to know that we are fulfilling the purpose for which we are on earth. All other standards of success - *wealth, power, position, knowledge, and friendships* - grow tiny and hollow if we do not satisfy this deeper longing."[57] I love the way the old hymn puts it:

> "I am resolved no longer to linger,
>   charmed by the world's delight;
> Things that are higher, things that are nobler,
>   These have allured my sight.
> I am resolved to enter the kingdom,
>   leaving the paths of sin;
> Friends may oppose me, foes may beset me;
>   Still I will enter in.
> I am resolved, and who will go with me?
>   Come, friends, without delay.
> Taught by the Bible, led by the Spirit,
>   We'll walk the heavenly way."
>
> Palmer Hartsough, 1896

That Oh Most Dangerous Prayer

As a young man in the first few furlongs of my lifelong journey with Jesus, the inimitable Jack Taylor, pastor and revival preacher, took me under his wing and taught me a prayer that I have never forgotten. It is a prayer every person can pray; indeed, a prayer every person *should* pray. However, I must warn you - it is a dangerous prayer.

It is simple, yet profound; specific, and yet comprehensive. It contains both a humble plea, as well as an audacious faith. This prayer is not likely to be prayed by people who are ambiguous about pleasing God, and it certainly will never find a voice among those who are always concerned about pleasing man.

Nevertheless, it is a prayer that *must* be prayed.

But, as I said, it is dangerous. Dangerous because it is irreversible; it will most certainly be answered by God, even though at times you will wish you'd never prayed it. Once God hears this prayer rise from your heart, the inevitable answer is set in motion – and all future cries to the contrary will fall as duds to the floor.

OK, I've given you fair warning. You now proceed at your own risk. I must caution you, however, that merely *reading* this prayer may be misconstrued by God as you actually praying it. So, if there is any measure of cowardice in you stop right now! Do not proceed!!

But for those who are faithful and courageous, and who hunger for God to use your life in extraordinary ways to make a difference in this world – here's that oh, most dangerous prayer:

"Lord Jesus, do in me anything You need to do, so that You can do through me everything You want to do. Amen."

Did you read it? Powerful, isn't it? Can you see how life-changing a simple prayer like that can be? Well, now I need to confess something to you. The very fact that you even *read* those words - that your mind actually formed them as a thought and said them inside your head - was taken by God as an actual prayer! It's too late to back out now; He thought you were praying, and the answer is already on the way!

Seeing we have come this far together, I should go ahead and give you one more dangerous prayer - what harm can it do now? I was also taught this prayer from dear Jack. One would think I would have learned my lesson by now, and found a way to avoid all contact and conversation with the fellow.

But he is sneaky. Right in the middle of an innocent, doting conversation - BAM! He smacks you right between the eyes. Let me show you what I mean - here's the other dangerous prayer he taught me:

"Dear Lord, please change my mind over every issue upon which You and I do not see eye to eye."

I tried to warn you. But you kept reading. So there you have it. The Lord heard your inner thoughts when you read those two prayers, and He has now officially undertaken the happy assignment of answering you.

What else can I say except, "Get ready for a life filled with WOW!"

Chapter Fifteen

Every Story Ends in *"Wow!"*

The premise of this final chapter is simple enough: Once Jesus becomes involved, every life story ends in *"Wow!"* Even yours; and that's the point of this book.

Someone said, "One may indeed be too big for God to use, but no one is ever too small." History abounds with example after example of those whose lives fill us with wonder over how God has used them. And, now it's your turn.

The prophet Daniel wrote:

"The people who know their God shall prove themselves strong and shall stand firm and do great exploits; they shall prevail valiantly." (see Daniel 11:32)

The backdrop for this splendid display of moral courage and social action was a time when deceit and flattery from political leaders had seduced the mindless masses into settling for a meaningless existence.

Sounds a lot like our world today, doesn't it? And *that's* when the people of God appear the brightest - "blameless and harmless, the sons of God without rebuke, in the midst of a crooked and perverse nation, among whom you shine as lights" (Philippians 2:15).

Is it possible, my friend, that God is calling you out of the comfort of a convenient life into a contest for truth and justice; an epic battle against the encroaching powers of darkness, which are stalking our homes, our schools, our courts, our market places, and our churches? Is it possible that you're the one who can stop the plague? All it takes is the right man at the right time. An example from the world of college football comes to mind.

During the 1990 season, the Colorado Buffaloes were in Austin, trailing the Texas Longhorns late in the third quarter, down 19-14. The Longhorns were marching with the ball, about to score another touchdown, which would have buried the Buffaloes. Eric Bieniemy, the short powerhouse running back for Colorado, huddled the huge offensive linemen together on the sidelines, and seemed to explode in a burst of enthusiasm, challenging them to turn things around.

The third quarter ended and the game paused for a TV timeout as the players moved to the other end of the field. The Texas home crowd cheered their team during the break. I could tell by the looks on their faces that the Longhorns felt that they were about to score the winning play.

But then something happened that I had never seen before, or since. As our beleaguered defensive players were walking slowly to the other end, our offensive players walked on the field during the break and began encouraging them. At Bieniemy's urging, the offense challenged the eleven guys on defense to hold Texas from scoring. "Get us the ball back, and we will beat these guys!" Bieniemy shouted. And he *meant* it.

It was exhilarating to see the empowering effect of those few moments. Our defense took heart and, with renewed determination, charged down to the other end of the field. They stood their ground and held Texas to a field goal. Colorado received the kick-off, marched down and scored right away. Then we held the Longhorns to three and out for the first time in the game, and got the ball back. Once again we drove for the go-ahead touchdown, which turned out to be the winning score.

Colorado went on to a ten game winning streak, including a victory against Notre Dame in the 1991 Orange Bowl for the National Championship. The defining moment of that season happened during the break between the third and fourth quarter of a game; a game whose outcome was still hanging in the balance.

The significance of this story is that one guy can make a difference, when he cares enough to do so. The infectious influence of a positive and affirming individual can turn the course of any campaign from defeat to victory. One guy like that can make a difference and change things for the better.

As someone once said, "It only takes a spark to get a fire going." So, are you ready to light things up, Sparky?

A small lad with five fish and two loaves of bread became the featured player in one of the greatest miracles Jesus ever performed. "What is this among so many," the doubting disciples asked.

You may be wondering something similar about yourself. "Who am I, that God would use me? What can I offer that would make any difference in today's world?" But don't count yourself out. The miracle worker from Galilee can still impact multitudes with the simple faith of a single boy. Dare to believe it and then take the risk of stepping up to the royal call upon your life.

"Who am I, that God would use me?"

Arthur Hugh Clough said it best in his little poem –

"Say not, 'The struggle naught availeth;
the labor and the toils are vain.
The enemy shrinks not, nor faileth.
As things have been, so they remain.'

For if hopes be dupes, then fears be liars.
It may be even now, your comrades
in yon smoke concealed, chase the fliers
- and, but for you, possess the field.'[58]

Your part matters far more than perhaps you may even realize; for you could be the voice that turns the battle, the man that makes the difference; your life can be the story that ends in, *"Wow!"*

When the Gadarene returned to his hometown and began telling the story of a Savior's power over darkness, the astounded crowds could only say, *"Wow!"*

When Paul returned to Jerusalem as a persecutor turned preacher, the disciples who had languished under his fierce harassment could only respond with one word, *"Wow!"*

When Peter, James and John saw the grace of God transcend Jewish boundaries and include Gentiles in so great a salvation, the only thing they could say was, *"Wow!"*

On the dreadful Isle of Patmos, the day after his extraordinary revelation, John surely looked at his fellow inmates and exclaimed, *"Wow!"*

Down through history, story after story has been written, each one tracing the wonder of God's amazing grace unleashed in the lives of men and women all around the world. In unison their voices rise in one great chorus, *"Wow!"*

Braveheart Moments

My friend, Coach Bill McCartney said "Wow!" more than any man I've ever met. "Big dreams create the magic that stirs men's souls to greatness!" he would often say. And nobody ever had bigger dreams than "Billy Mac from Hackensack." As a young assistant coach at Michigan, he was challenged at a FCA breakfast and gave his heart to Jesus.

From that point forward Mac was consumed with a passion to reach men for Christ. And God began blessing his efforts in extraordinary ways. Not only in his work as a college football coach, with Michigan and then Colorado, but especially once he stepped up to launch Promise Keepers (PK), a national men's movement that has impacted literally millions of men around the world with the life-changing power of the Gospel. *Wow!*

As one of the first PK stadium events drew toward a close, Coach Mac issued a provocative challenge to over fifty thousand men. "You guys need to love, honor, and support your *pastor*! He walks a lonely road, and is often under constant attack, not only from the devil, but from disgruntled church members as well. Let him know how much you care!"

Then something happened, which to this day is one of the single, most memorable things I have personally ever witnessed. The men in the stadium erupted in a *Braveheart* cheer, as a few thousand pastors made their way down to the stadium floor.

Some guys even hoisted their pastor on their shoulders, like football teams lift a winning coach, and carried him down out of the stands to the field. Men were shouting, pastors were weeping, and the devil was on the run in Boulder, Colorado! *Wow!*

On another occasion two guys drove across country from California to attend *Stand in the Gap*, the historic PK event held on the National Mall in Washington DC, on October 4, 1997. They passed a hitchhiker on the way and decided to turn around and offer him a ride. The offer carried one condition - that he would go along with them to the event. The guy agreed. What else was he going to do?

They talked as they rode together, and the homeless man told them his story. He was raised in Fayetteville, Arkansas, and had married when he was only nineteen. Within a year he had a son, and felt overwhelmed with all the responsibility. So he simply ran away. That was twenty-two years ago; and he had been aimlessly drifting about ever since.

You can imagine the sheer amazement of these guys when they arrived at the event in Washington and saw more than a million men swarming about the Mall. As they made their way through the teeming crowd, they came upon a group of guys all wearing bright red tee shirts, with matching ball caps. They were from a church in *Fayetteville*. Was this a coincidence?

Oh, more than you realize! For the thing that no one could have ever even imagined was that the youth pastor who had brought these Fayetteville guys to the Mall, was none other than this homeless man's abandoned son, now grown up and serving God!

So, there they stood, face-to-face, and embraced in a long overdue bond of love and forgiveness in the presence of the Lord. And, when all was said and done, the dad returned home to Fayetteville with his son. *Wow!*

Would you bear with me as I tell just one more story? It's my personal favorite. I mentioned earlier that Promise Keepers had asked me to preach the Gospel at the event in

Washington. As I was closing my message that day, I invited those who were watching by television to join in along with the men who were responding to Christ at the event. "You can stand up right there in your living room," I said, "and raise your arms in surrender to Christ; trusting Him to be your Lord and Savior as we pray."

A few weeks later, in California for a church conference, I went out to eat with a group of the guys. While we were at our table, a young man walked over and asked, "Are you the guy who preached the Gospel at Stand in the Gap?"

"Yes, I am."

"Would you mind if I told you something that God did?"

"Not at all," I replied, "Please tell me."

I was deeply touched by what this young man said next. Even now I can hardly talk about it without crying. His father, a minister, had an affair with his secretary and it resulted in a shameful and bitter divorce. His mother turned away from the Faith, seething with unforgiveness.

A few years later she remarried a staunch atheist and they had a daughter together. They resolved to shield her from any exposure whatsoever to religion of any kind, and they required this young man, her brother, to comply with their wishes and not try to evangelize her.

On that Saturday morning that seven year-old-girl was unsupervised in the living room, watching television and channel-surfing. Her dad was out of town and mom was at the store. Her brother, accustomed to hearing cartoon noise coming from the living room, noticed a strange quietness and decided to go and check on her. She had found the CSPAN broadcast of Stand In the Gap.

He walked in at the moment I was extending the invitation to those who were watching. And there was his little sister, standing up with her arms lifted to Jesus, asking Him to be her Savior! *Wow!*

He Saved the Best for Now

Are you beginning to see what I mean? Once Jesus becomes involved, every story ends in, *Wow!* This means that *your* story is headed for glory, now that your heart is opened to His presence and power.

At the wedding in Cana, Jesus turned the water into a wine of such exquisite quality, that the people exclaimed, "He saved the best for now!" How exactly did this miracle happen? We are told that Jesus had been invited to the wedding, and He came with His disciples. Then, once they ran out of wine, Jesus stepped in and made the difference. They did what He told them to do, and the miracle occurred. He will do the same for you, if you will faithfully do as He says.

One memory I have from early childhood, before I was placed in the orphanage, is that of my mother walking in on me while I was in the midst of mischief. I had taken a pair of scissors and began cutting the flower patterns out of the sofa. "What

"What on earth are you doing for Heaven's sake?"

on earth are you doing?" she exclaimed. And then, in the same breath, having seen for herself what it was, she said, "Oh, for heaven's sake!!" Now, to a three year old boy that sounded like one complete question to me.

And that's the question I pose to you now – *"What on earth are you doing for heaven's sake?"*

A needy world waits on tiptoe to see what you will do. Our eyes strain for an unrestricted view and our hearts long for some heroic act. And our breath, held in anticipation of something great that you will do, awaits for that singular moment when we may all say together, *"Wow!"*

Oh, please do not disappoint us.

You might still be wondering, "Who am I that such things as you suggest should be expected of me?" Well, honestly, you're *nobody* - just like the rest of us! But Jesus is *Somebody*, and He has done everything necessary to ensure our success in completing His mission in this world.

I love the way Jamie Buckingham said it, "All the holy men seem to have gone off and died. There's no one left but us sinners to carry on the ministry." Sinners saved by grace, and empowered to do God's will!

Let me highlight four great provisions which are at your full disposal; and which, if you avail yourself of these things, will undoubtedly help you serve the Lord faithfully and completely; as a man released from the prison your father built, living an extraordinary life, and becoming yet another story that ends in, *"Wow!"*

Provision #1 - The Power of God's Word

The first provision for our transforming journey is the Word of God. "All Scripture is inspired by God and is useful for teaching the truth, rebuking error, correcting faults, and giving instruction for right living, so that the person who serves God may be fully qualified and equipped to do every kind of good deed." (2 Timothy 3:16, Good News Bible)

That about says it all. Several years ago, in the front pages of one of those large Family Bibles, I found this remarkable summary of the Bible's comprehensive value:

Thïs Book contains the mind of God, the state of man, the way of salvation, the doom of sinners, and the happiness of believers. Its doctrines are holy, its precepts are binding, its histories are true, and it decisions are immutable. Read it to be wise, believe it to be safe, and practice it to be holy. It contains light to direct you, food to support you, and comfort to cheer you. It is the traveler's map, the pilgrim's staff, the pilot's compass, the soldier's sword, and the Christian's charter. Here Paradise is restored, Heaven opened, and the Gates of Hell disclosed. Christ is its Grand Subject, our good its design, and the Glory of God its end. It should fill the memory, rule the heart, and guide the feet. Read it slowly, frequently, and prayerfully. It is a mine of wealth, a paradise of glory, and a river of pleasure. It is given you in life, will be opened at the judgment, and be remembered forever. It involves the highest responsibility, rewards the greatest labor, and condemns all who trifle with its holy contents. This volume is the Word of GOD."

I can tell you from almost forty years of personal experience that the best and surest thing you can do to enrich your life is to *devour* the Bible. Read it, study it, pray it, dream it, sing it, talk it, live it, and teach it to others. Your heart will rejoice, your eyes will be enlightened, your soul will be purified, your mind will grow, and your life will be remarkably blessed. But there's still more!

You will also discover, as you spend prayerful time in the Bible, that you actually increase the vocabulary with which God may speak to you in situations throughout the day. You will learn not only God's *word*, but also His *ways*.

Your sense of discernment will sharpen, as will your sensitivity to His still, small voice, which gives you timely guidance, answers the difficult questions your face, helps you make the right decisions, and emboldens you to do the right thing at the right time. And this brings us to the next provision the Lord has made for you.

Provision #2 - Friendship with the Holy Spirit

One of history's unsung heroes is a man named Ludwig Nommensen, a German Lutheran missionary sent to Sumatra in 1862. He focused his attention on the Batak people of the Indonesian interior. While he met with typical difficulties for the first few years, his unflagging zeal ultimately turned the tide. By the time of his death in 1918 at the age of eighty-four, the church he had started numbered over 180,000 members, with 34 Batak pastors and 788 teacher-preachers assisting in the work. Its prevailing influence lasts to this day.

A turning point came early in Ludwig's labors when a prominent chief of the Batak asked him a question.

"We, too, have laws that say we must not steal, nor take our neighbor's wife, nor bear false witness," the chief said. "So how does what you teach differ from what we already know?"

"My Master doesn't merely tell us what to do," he answered, "He also gives the power to do it."

The chief was startled. "Can you teach my people that?"

"God will do it if they ask for it and listen to His Word," Ludwig replied.

So for six months Nommensen taught the Batak about the power of God, and friendship with the Holy Spirit. At the end of that time the chief said, "Stay, your law is better than ours. Ours tells us what we ought to do. Your God says, 'Come, I will walk with you and give you strength to do the good thing.'"

And the rest, as they say, is history.

God will also walk with you, and give you the strength to do the good thing. Jesus promised us that we would not be left as orphans, but that we would have a constant friend who would walk with us, talk to us, teach us, guide us, empower us and help us every day in every way. That *Friend* is the Holy Spirit.

The simple definition of a friend is "one attached to another by affection or esteem." We rightly imagine that our friendship with the Holy Spirit is based upon our affection and esteem for Him, but friendship is never one-sided. Perhaps you have never considered that the Holy Spirit is also attached to you by the strong affection and high esteem that He has for *you*! Has it ever occurred to you just how much the Holy Spirit actually *enjoys* being with you?

Oh, but don't let it go to your head - for there are many, many others He feels this way about. And He wants to introduce you to them, so that they can get to know you like He knows you; even as you get to know them. And this brings me to the next provision Christ has made for us.

Provision #3 - A Growing Circle of True Friends

Pentecost, the day when Heaven came to earth, accomplished two things that have redefined our world. First, there was fusion; and then there was empowerment.

Back in the earliest days of civilized man's heavenly aspirations, a knucklehead named Nimrod thought he would build a tower whose height reached into heaven itself. We know it as the Tower of Babel. We also know the legendary story of how God disrupted the building program by confusing the language of the people.

Once communication breaks down, relationships are over, and all cooperative projects fall unfinished. *Babel* - even today we use the word to describe a confusing sound of words or noises. The word *confusion* means to mix together things that do not belong together. In the case of Babylon, there was an arrogant man trying to become God's equal - that is *confusion*.

There is a beauty in *community* that the world longs to experience.

Fusion, on the other hand, means "to melt so as to merge." This occurred on the day of Pentecost when a mighty, rushing wind rocked Jerusalem as tongues of fire rested upon the waiting disciples. God *fused* together a community of spiritually gifted men and women to love and serve one another in the beauty of holiness. We call this emerging community, which now is global, the Church.

There is a beauty in community that the world longs to experience. When one is a part of a growing circle of true friends, he or she will experience acceptance of who they really are, affirmation of what God has given them to do, and accountability that keeps them on the right path. But there's more!

The Lord didn't simply fuse us together with one another; He joined us inseparably to Himself as well! And in so doing unleashed the power of heaven into each one of our lives. Now, He wants to release that very power through our lives to a world still in need of a Savior's redeeming love and grace. Which brings me to the fourth provision God has made for us.

Provision #4 - The Upward Call

Many people meander through life as though it were a flea market. They browse the bins for the deal of a lifetime, only to come home with someone else's junk. Others are a bit more like the crazy rabbit in Alice's Wonderland, always on the go for something that is always somewhere else and never getting there.

Some people sit in the stands and watch others play the game and reassure themselves that they *could* do that if they wanted to. Others see a great opportunity and console themselves with a reflective sigh, "I *should* do that." But, of course they never do. And then there are those who wistfully say, "I *would* do that," hinting by their tone that it's somebody else's fault if they don't.

Could do, should do, and would do *never* do.

The only thing that works is when you find the thing that you *must* do. God uses the inner pull of that upward call to tip the battle in your favor. There is a resolute power inherent in any great work; once you become involved in such an enterprise you are virtually unstoppable.

When Nehemiah undertook the great challenge of rebuilding the walls of Jerusalem, he had enemies who constantly opposed him and sought his ruin. First they tried ridicule; it didn't work. Then they made overt threats of hostility; it was, as they say, water off a duck's back to Nehemiah.

Next they attempted covert sabotage, but he foiled their plot. Nothing fazed him. Finally they tried the *diplomatic* approach, seeking some sort of compromise. Nehemiah's answer stands to this day as one of the greatest closers in any conflict - "I am doing a great work," he said, "Why should the work stop while I come *down* to you?"[59]

His passion for answering the upward call minimized the effects of those who were always seeking to drag him down to their level. They lost; he won.

The apostle Paul said, "I press toward the goal for the prize of the upward call of God in Christ Jesus" (Phil 3:14). Notice the cooperative relationship here between God calling us upward and our pressing toward that goal. Both must work together in order to live a life that ends in *"Wow!"*

Have you ever taken a volleyball into a swimming pool, pushed it down into the water, and then tried to stand on it? Did you notice that the deeper you pushed the ball into the water, the greater the force it exerted to rise back up to the top?

There is an environment *inside* the ball that is foreign to the environment of the water, into which you are pressing it. The air inside the ball *belongs* with the air above the water, and it will press upward to return where it belongs. And that's the way it is with us as followers of Jesus. Something inside us *urges* us to the summit; it's the upward call.

Some merely drift along, hoping for a break here or there, and never intentionally exert themselves toward the better choice. But drifting will never get you to where you are supposed to be, for in life, as in nature, nothing ever drifts *upstream*.

The only exception to this happened in Texas during a freak flash flood.

The waters rose so quickly that people only had time to scurry to their rooftops. One man, a reporter, sat on the house watching the floodwaters sweep past. Cars, cows and cats and all kinds of things zipped by the house.

Suddenly something caught his eye. A $500 Stetson hat came floating down stream, just out of his reach. However, before it passed by, the hat stopped, turned around and floated back up stream. It then came back, stopped and turned back upstream again.

Amazed, the reporter said, "This is a miracle: it will be the lead story in my paper tomorrow!"

A woman sitting on the roof next door heard him and replied, "That's no miracle. It's just my husband Cecil. He said he was going to mow that lawn come hell or high water!"

Like I said, nothing ever drifts upstream. Left to ourselves we will not rise, but fall. However, God does not leave us to ourselves; He calls us upward. Something deep inside us is hooked to heaven; a tug on our hearts inclines us towards the higher way. As the old hymn says, "I'm pressing on the upward way; new heights I'm gaining everyday. Still, praying as I onward bound, 'Lord, plant my feet on higher ground!'"[60]

I pray that you will make that your quest from this day forward.

A Final Word

"He was a burning and a shining light" (John 5:35).

This lasting tribute was said of John the Baptist by none other than Jesus Himself. Moreover, Jesus also said, "I tell you the truth: Among those born of women there has not risen anyone greater than John the Baptist."

And then He added this promising word – "Yet he who is least in the kingdom of heaven is greater than he" (Matthew 11:11).

This means that each one of us may, like John, be a burning and shining light. We may live in such a manner as to receive the acclaim of the Lord Jesus.

> ## "The cost of shining is burning."
> Leonard Ravenhill

But there is a price to be paid. Years ago I heard the great revival preacher, Leonard Ravenhill, say, "The cost of shining is burning."

Many want the glow without the heat, but there can be no sparkle where there are not sparks. And, there can be no sparks where the hammer of God's word does not strike the anvil of our souls as the Holy Spirit forges Christ-like character in the metal of our lives.

The cost of shining is *burning*.

The disciples said, "Did not our heart burn within us while He talked with us along the way, and while He opened to us the Scriptures?" (Luke 24:32).

In yet another place the Bible asks, "Does not My word burn like fire?" says the LORD. "Is it not like a mighty hammer that smashes a rock to pieces?" (Jeremiah 23:29).

As we open ourselves to the igniting power of God's Word all within us that is wood, hay or stubble is consumed by its tireless flame. And then whatever remains deep in our hearts, and is yet hardened and unresponsive to God's Spirit, is busted loose by the mighty blow of God's hammer - His living word unleashed in our yielded lives.

Will you let the truth of God's unchanging Word have its way in your life? In your thoughts, your hopes, and your aspirations? In your opinions, your attitudes, and your behavior? In your family, your friendships, and your associations?

If you say yes, you will become a burning and shining light; and you will be counted great in the Kingdom of God.

Yield your heart to Christ and let Him be honored by the light of your ignited life. And He will say of you on that day, "This one was a burning and shining light."

It was a night I shall never forget. Praying in my prison cell during the chill of a Texas December, my heart was warmed by the power of a single verse of Scripture.

"Go home to your friends and tell them the great things the Lord has done for you, how He has had compassion on you." (Mark 5:19, KJV)

These are the words the Lord Jesus spoke to the liberated Gadarene, and sent him on his mission to the far reaches of his world.

These are also the words that God spoke to my heart all those years ago as I knelt in prayer inside my cell, asking if I could be set free from a Texas prison - *the prison my father built.*

I walked out of the prison and began telling my story to anybody who would listen. And now I've told my story to you.

This whole thing started with a question that I had to ask; and I think, as I now bring this to a close, that perhaps it should end with a question as well. Actually, it's more like a series of questions, which only you can answer. And there are so many who are waiting to hear what your answers will be. So, here is what I will ask you.

There's a well in the valley; do you dig it? There's a mountain in the hills; do you climb it? There's a song on your lips; do you sing it? There's a bell in the tower; do you ring it?

There is love in your heart; do you show it? There's a chance every day; do you blow it?
There's a life full of joy; do you live it?
There's a coin in your pocket; will you give it?

There's a reason you are here; do you know it?
There's a seed in your soul; will you grow it?
There's a calling on your life; do you hear it?
There's a time to take a stand; do you fear it?

There's a way to change the world; do you see it?
There's a dream that's locked away; will you free it? There's a word to be spoken; will you speak it?
There's a faith from above; will you keep it?

There's a truth to be told; will you tell it?
There is freedom in the air; can you smell it?
There's a path less traveled; will you take it? There is glory up in heaven; will you make it?

There's a door that's opened wide; will you enter? Will you cross the finish line as a winner?[61]

The story is told of how the great Leonardo Da Vinci had started work on a large canvas in his studio. A few of his students watched as he worked at it - choosing the subject, planning the perspective, sketching the outline, and applying the colors; all with his own inimitable genius.

Then he unexpectedly paused, the painting still unfinished, and summoned one of his students to step up and complete the work.

The student protested that he was unworthy and unable to complete the great painting that his master had begun. But Da Vinci answered, "Will not what I have done inspire you to do your very best?"

"Will not what I have done inspire you to do your very best?"

Do you think that Jesus might be saying a similar thing to you? He has generously provided everything you need to live a life that honors God and benefits others. Believe it, take hold of it, press on with it, and give us all cause to stand in celebration of the many great things the Lord does in you, to you, with you, and through you until the day of His return.

All through this book we have read of many individuals who heard God's voice and followed His leading. And in each instance they found the courage and power to do what He told them. As a result they experienced God's presence, and made a difference in their world. *Wow!*

Now it's *your* turn.

Throughout the entire process of compiling, writing, editing, re-writing, praying, and re-writing again; setting the whole thing aside for months, then dusting it off to see if it merits another look; editing yet again, and re-writing, and finally publishing the book for you to read - in all of this a single, over-riding objective has held my hopeful heart: *helping you experience God's Presence.*

In a sentence – my aim has been to help you learn to recognize how and when God is speaking to you, and to find the power and courage to do whatever He is leading you to do. I trust I have been successful.

My story serves only as a backdrop for you to discover your own story; to know the love of God and to experience the many ways He uses to make Himself known to you – and also *through* you to others.

Your life is a story yet being written by the pen of God. The end has not yet been pressed. You are on a most excellent adventure. Each day holds promise for a new series of encounters with God's love and faithfulness, which will help you to stop believing the many lies that have bombarded your soul and diminished your potential.

And by His grace, so generously supplied, you can walk in the freedom that comes with personal responsibility - and live each day giving freely to others what has been given to you.

May you fare well on your journey with Jesus to that City, whose builder and maker is God. I will see you at the Summit – and there in the Lord's presence, we will share together in the grand celebration of eternal life.

And now, I suppose that the only thing left to say is, *"Wow!"*

End Notes

[1] Isaac Newton, *Letter to Robert Hooke, February 5, 1675*
[2] Robert Burton, *Anatomy of Melancholy*
    (pt. III, sect. II, memb. 5, subsec. 1)
[3] See 2 Samuel 12:10
[4] See Exodus 20:5,6
[5] Jeremiah 1:5, The Message, ©1995 NavPress
[6] 1 Corinthians 13:11
[7] 1 Corinthians 1:27
[8] Rocky Mountain News, September 5,1989
[9] 1 Chronicles 16:22
[10] 1 John 2:19
[11] Romans 16:17
[12] Numbers 32:23
[13] Matthew 18:6
[14] Baxter, J. Sidlow, Explore the Book – Volume 3, (Zondervan Publishing House, Grand Rapids, MI, 1966), p. 259
[15] Genesis 2:18, KJV
[16] Charles Lamb, *The Essays of Elia* (Charles Scribner's Sons, 1900) p. 90-91
[17] GospelCom.Net: *Lonely But Never Alone*, p. 7.
[18] Hosea 4:17
[19] Francis J. Crosby, *Pass Me Not, O Gentle Savior*, 1898. Public domain.
[20] Albert Jewell (editor), *Spirituality and Aging* (Jessica Kingsley Publisher, 1998) p. 19
[21] Romans 3:23
[22] Acts 17:30-31, NKJV © 1982 by Thomas Nelson, Inc.
[23] John 3:16
[24] John 14:6
[25] Philippians 2:8-11
[26] Acts 4:12
[27] 1 Timothy 2:4-6, The Living Bible
[28] Romans 5:19
[29] 1 Corinthians 15:22
[30] 2 Corinthians 5:17
[31] Romans 5:8
[32] Romans 8:32
[33] Psalm 14:2,3
[34] Hebrews 4:15

[35] Romans 6:23

[36] Romans 5:20

[37] Joshua 24:15

[38] 2 Peter 3:9

[39] 1 Timothy 2:4

[40] Romans 10:13

[41] Romans 10:9

[42] 1 Samuel 17:55

[43] *When Did I Become a Man*, by James Ryle, 1991

[44] Martin Luther King (James Washington, editor), *A Testament of Hope: The Essential Writings and Speeches of Martin Luther King, Jr.* (New York, NY: Harper One Publishers, 1990) p. 270

[45] 2 Timothy 1:7

[46] H. Ernest Nichol, *We've a Story to tell the Nations* (London: 1896). Public domain.

[47] John 8:32

[48] Psalm 18:25

[49] Galatians 5:16

[50] Isaiah 30:21

[51] Jean Darby, *Dwight D. Eisenhower* (Lerner Pub, 2004) p. 99

[52] Joseph Morris and St. Claire Adams, *It Can Be Done; Poems of Inspiration* (New York; Sully, 1929) p. 7

[53] Go to www.bezandoho.com for more information

[54] Go to www.e-sword.net to download the Bible program and lots of resources!

[55] Dwight Eisenhower, Presidential Speech, April 2, 1957

[56] William Paul McKay and Ken Abraham, *Billy: The Untold Story of a Young Billy Graham* (Nashville, TN; Thomas Nelson Publishers, 2008) p. 257

[57] Os Guinness, *The Call* (Nashville, TN; Thomas Nelson Publishers, 1998)

[58] Richard Garnett, Leon Vallee, and Alois Brandl (Editors) *The Universal Anthology V11: A Collection Of The Best Literature, Ancient, Mediaeval And Modern* (Kessinger Pub, 1899) p. 47

[59] Nehemiah 6:3

[60] Johnson Oatman, Jr, *Higher Ground*, 1898. Public domain.

[61] *Questions Only You Can Answer*, by James Ryle, 2008